Response to Intervention (RtI) for Teachers

for Teachers

Classroom Instructional Problem Solving

Response to Intervention (RtI) for Teachers
Classroom Instructional Problem Solving

Mary E. Little
University of Central Florida

LOVE PUBLISHING COMPANY®
Denver • London • Sydney

 Published by Love Publishing Company
P.O. Box 22353
Denver, Colorado 80222
www.lovepublishing.com

Library of Congress Catalog Card Number 2008921128

Copyright © 2009 by Love Publishing Company
Printed in the United States of America
ISBN 978-0-89108-338-2

Dedication

Sincere thanks to D'Ann Rawlinson and the
teachers in Florida, who inspire with their classroom
instructional problem solving, continuous learning,
collaboration, and reflection.
Your knowledge, dedication, and commitment to
improved learning for all students make all the difference!

Contents

Preface

In classrooms and schools across the United States, recent state and federal mandates and requirements have increased the emphasis on accountability for high-quality instruction and interventions for all students, with and without disabilities. In addition, data-driven instruction and interventions must be developed, implemented, and monitored prior to referrals for additional services, including special education, for individual students. Response to Intervention (RtI) has been developed as a model for preventing academic failure among students, as well as for identifying students with learning disabilities (Fuchs & Fuchs, 2006b; IDEA, 2004). RtI is defined as a systematic and data-based method for identifying, defining, and resolving students' academic and behavioral difficulties through a problem-solving process that uses the skills of professionals from different disciplines to develop and evaluate intervention plans that significantly improve the performance of students (Fuchs, 2003).

In addition, within the last few years, classroom instructional decision making (also referred to as action research, critical inquiry, and problem solving) has developed as a means for school improvement and professional development (Calhoun, 2002), as well as a process to describe the impact of professional development related to student learning (Guskey, 2000).

Response to Intervention (RtI) for Teachers: Classroom Instructional Problem Solving is an interactive, practical resource for teachers and other educators to actively participate in the problem-solving instructional process within the Response to Intervention model in classrooms and schools to improve achievement for all students. These resources provide teachers with a step-by-step approach to conducting classroom instructional problem solving (action research), including descriptions of each phase, reflection activities, planning forms, and concrete, real-life examples of action research. This instructional problem-solving process will be described within the context of the RtI process. The examples, planning forms, charts, and case studies included in this book will be applicable to all educators interested in using data for classroom instructional decision making. Action research is a cyclical and continuous process. However, for the purpose of describing and modeling the process in these resources, the tiers of the RtI model and phases of action research will be described in a linear fashion.

This workbook will provide teachers, professional developers, teacher leaders, literacy coaches, school and district administrators, university professors, and other educators with practical and proven resources, examples, planning forms, case studies, and related materials to facilitate the data-based, problem-solving process in classrooms within the RtI framework. This process mirrors the teaching and assessing process as part of effective instruction. Evaluating the impact of teaching through student results has been a part of this instructional cycle for years. However, given the current focus on accountability for improved student results for all students, this need to describe, assess, and quantify student results as related to instruction, differentiation, and intensive interventions within the process of Response to Intervention is paramount and increasing. This book will meet this need through a practical, teacher-focused process approach, based upon the most current research, legislation, and policies, while providing evidence-based resources in both instruction and assessments for use in classrooms.

This book can be used in many different contexts. These resources may be used as a (1) teaching tool for educators and schools interested in learning about the process of instructional decision making (problem solving) within the RtI process, (2) part of the special education identification and IEP development process, (3) learning guide for students in a college course, or (4) resource for educators working towards certification, reading endorsement, National Board Certification, and as an alternative to individual professional development plans within school districts that require evidence of student learning.

Acknowledgement

The author acknowledges the Florida Department of Education, Bureau of Exceptional Education and Student Services, for its support for action research within teacher professional development to ensure improved student learning in Florida.

Introduction

Response to Intervention for Teachers: Classroom Instructional Problem Solving

In classrooms and schools across the United States, recently legislated federal and state requirements have increased the emphasis on accountability for high-quality instruction and interventions for all students, both with and without disabilities. The purpose is to improve all students' achievement, which is continuously monitored by teachers and other school professionals through ongoing assessments in classrooms. Data-driven instruction and interventions must be developed, implemented, and monitored before referrals for additional services, including special education for identified students.

Response to Intervention (RtI) offers a model for preventing academic failure among students and identifying students with learning disabilities (Fuchs & Fuchs, 2006a; Denton, 2006; IDEA, 2004). RtI is a systematic data-based method for identifying, defining, and resolving students' academic or behavioral difficulties. As a problem-solving process, RtI uses the skills of professionals from different disciplines to develop and evaluate intervention plans that significantly improve the performance of students (Fuchs, Mock, Morgan, & Young, 2002).

Increased systematic use of instructional problem solving, accompanied by a process for determining eligibility for special education and other supplemental services, allows integration of instruction and interventions for the specific, data-driven needs of individual students. As Batsche and colleagues (2006) note, an instructional problem-solving model can

- provide a process to identify and use various instructional and intensive interventions;
- facilitate increased implementation of evidence-based instructional methods, strategies, and resources;

1

- document student progress through continuous progress monitoring;
- and increase the speed and efficiency of services that improve student performance.

Research suggests that, to continuously monitor student progress to realize the benefits for improved student achievement, teachers need information on the process of data-based classroom instructional problem solving, as well as definitions and examples of evidence-based instruction and definitions and examples of classroom assessments (Flugum & Reschly, 1994). *RtI for Teachers* has been written with these needs in mind.

Within the last few years, classroom instructional problem solving (also referred to as action research, critical inquiry, and classroom decision making) has become both a tool for school improvement and professional development (Calhoun, 2002) and a process for describing the impact of professional development related to student learning (Guskey, 2000; Guskey & Sparks, 1996; Killion, 2005). In this book, the term "classroom instructional problem solving" refers to the decision-making process teachers use to solve instructional (academic and behavioral) issues, concerns, and problems within their classrooms. Teachers and school professionals may invoke this process for several reasons:

1. To continuously monitor student learning for adjustments to teaching, methods, resources, and so on
2. To collect evidence of student learning for accountability mandated by the school, district, or state
3. To aggregate and summarize achievement data for additional professional purposes, such as National Board Certification or university courses
4. To use in program-level decision making within school-wide initiatives for intervention teams, determining eligibility for special education services, or to determine other necessary instructional and intervention services needed,
5. To complete classroom research related to specific classroom instructional techniques or processes (action research)

In action research, teachers systematically reflect on their practice and make changes to their instruction based on careful analysis of current classroom performance of their students (Dana & Yendol-Silva, 2003; FDOE, 2004b; Little, 2003; Sagor, 2005). In traditional research, researchers study the teachers. In action research, however, the teachers become the primary researchers, studying ways to improve student learning in their classrooms. As researchers, teachers are essential to analyzing instructional concerns and individual student issues within their classrooms. After collecting information related to an identified problem, teachers decide on the content, methods, or strategies that would best resolve the identified instructional concern. By continuously monitoring the results of those decisions, teachers determine the effectiveness of the decisions with respect to the desired goals for the students. This interactive, dynamic process approach to instructional problem solving requires teachers to know about data collection, evidence-based instructional practices and resources, and both informal and diagnostic assessments.

Response to Intervention (RtI) for Teachers: Classroom Instructional Problem Solving is an interactive, practical resource for teachers and other educators. *RtI for Teachers* reveals how to actively participate in the problem-solving instructional process by using a model of the RtI process in classrooms and schools. The RtI model and phases of instructional problem solving are cyclical and continuous; however, they are described in a linear fashion within this book.

The resources contained in *RtI for Teachers* provide a step-by-step approach to classroom instructional problem solving (action research), including descriptions of each phase, reflection activities, planning forms, and concrete, real-life examples, all aimed at improving achievement for all students. The examples, planning forms, charts, and case studies included in this book are relevant to any educator who is interested in using data for instructional problem solving in classrooms and schools.

RtI for Teachers addresses the need to provide teachers, professional developers, teacher leaders, literacy coaches, school and district administrators, university professors, and other educators with practical and proven resources. These resources are all designed to facilitate the data-based, problem-solving process in classrooms within the RtI framework—a process that mirrors the teaching and assessing process as part of effective instruction.

Evaluating the impact of teaching through student results has been a part of the instructional cycle for years. However, given the current focus on accountability for improved results for all students, the need to describe, assess, and quantify student results as related to instruction, differentiation, or intensive interventions within the process of RtI is paramount and increasing. *RtI for Teachers* meets this need. Through its practical, teacher-focused process approach based on current research, legislation, and policies, *RtI for Teachers* offers evidence-based resources in both instruction and assessments for use in classrooms and schools.

CHAPTER 1

WHY? The Rationale for Classroom Instructional Problem Solving

Overview

This chapter presents the rationale for teachers, literacy coaches, curriculum specialists, and other educators to be actively accountable within their classrooms through the Response to Intervention (RtI) process. As Guskey (2000) notes, the classroom and school levels are where the action is, making these levels the best sources for identifying educational problems and issues. This chapter calls for teachers, literacy coaches, and other classroom- and school-based educators to consider why instructional problem solving is so important—that is, how it meets the instructional needs of all of their students. In addition, the chapter provides an overview of the mandated problem-solving process of RtI, including definitions, tiers, and classroom implications. The RtI framework and problem-solving process provide the overarching structure for this discussion.

Reflection Questions:

- *What is Response to Intervention (RtI)?*
- *Why do I need to know about the RtI process?*
- *What is my role within the RtI process?*
- *How is instructional problem solving related to RtI?*

"Almost 30 years of research and experiences has demonstrated that the education of students with disabilities can be made more effective by providing incentives for whole school approaches."

~ (IDEA 2004)

Response to Intervention (RtI) is a systematic, data-based method for identifying, defining, and resolving students' academic or behavioral difficulties using collaborative, school-wide, problem-solving approaches. As a proactive and prevention-focused approach, it relies on instructional problem solving within classrooms and schools, and it encourages teams of educators to develop dynamic instructional plans to address academic or behavioral concerns of individual students within general-education classrooms. RtI focuses on using evidence-based instructional approaches, resources, and strategies within the classroom, while continuously monitoring student learning that results from the teacher's varied instructional methods. Instructional problem solving, based on student data, is the framework for the RtI model. Since the goal is to increase achievement for all students, classroom teachers are the primary participants in the RtI process. RtI's comprehensive and continuous process, however, may include other educators (e.g., the reading teacher, speech-language pathologist, school psychologist) on the school-based team to help identify and participate in possible solutions for instructional concerns of students.

The core concepts of RtI include critical elements of effective teaching which rest on evidence-based instructional methods, resources, and strategies in instruction and assessment. These core concepts include:

1. high-quality, evidence-based instruction in general education settings for all students;
2. continuous progress monitoring of student learning related to curricular standards;
3. differentiation of instruction to meet learning needs of all students;
4. universal screening and data collection for all students in classrooms;
5. high-quality, evidence-based interventions in general settings for all students;
6. continuous progress monitoring of student learning resulting from instruction and interventions; and
7. school-wide problem solving and classroom instructional support.

Teachers and other educators are cognizant of many core concepts necessary for implementation of RtI. However, the emphasis today is on a *systematic* process to ensure success for all students—an emphasis arising from the changing processes for identifying students with disabilities, especially those with learning disabilities in reading. Currently driving changes in legislation and procedures are issues related to misdiagnosis, over- and under-representation of minorities, costs and time needed for assessment, and the "wait-to-fail" aspects of some procedures. Most importantly, a proactive, prevention model of classroom instructional problem solving, based on student data, serves as the catalyst for the current legislation and mandates of RtI. Specific legislative policies and background research provided the underpinnings for the core concepts of the current RtI model.

Reflection Question:

• *What do I know about legislation that affects my classroom teaching?*

Important Legislation

In the current context of standards-based reform and heightened accountability for school performance by all students, RtI has underpinnings in previous legislation and initiatives in special education. Recent reauthorization of two important and related pieces of federal legislation establish the framework for RtI: Title 1 of the Elementary and Secondary Education Act as the No Child Left Behind Act (2002) and the Individuals with Disabilities Education Improvement Act (2004).

No Child Left Behind

In 2001, Congress passed the No Child Left Behind Act (NCLB) as a compromise bill to address issues identified through a number of education reform proposals. The law intended to hold school districts accountable for the learning of all students. To achieve this outcome, the legislation included two interrelated components: accountability standards for student learning and the quality of teachers.

The demands for accountability of NCLB include participation by all students in assessment procedures to ensure that every subgroup of children, including students with disabilities (SWDs), improves with each successive year, with the goal of every child reaching proficiency by 2012 (Pascopella, 2003). Towards that end, NCLB requires a system of accountability to measure whether schools and districts are making adequate yearly progress (AYP) to ensure that all students, including students with disabilities, meet or exceed the proficiency level on the state assessments. NCLB requires states to develop educational programs, identify programs and resources, and support instructional pratices, based on scientific studies, to be used within classrooms. Language in this legislation mandates accountability for *all* students, and federal and state regulations clarify specific accommodations and modifications to the procedures to be used for initially assessing students with the most significant cognitive disabilities as well as AYP. These regulations describe

- standardized and acceptable accommodations and modifications (as determined on a case-by-case basis by the members of an individual educational plan, or IEP),
- the use of alternate achievement standards in determination of AYP, and
- criteria for proficient or advanced scores, provided the alternate achievement standards counted toward AYP at the district and state level are not applied to more than 1.0% of all students assessed.

Because NCLB focuses on prevention, the least intrusive methods necessary are used to meet the goals of established student outcomes. Policy grounded in a prevention model requires evidence-based reading instruction as the core curriculum, but also includes provisions for increasingly explicit and intensive instruction for students who do not respond to initial instruction.

Individuals With Disabilities Improvement Education Act

Since initial passage of legislation in 1975, the quality of education provided to students with disabilities has improved significantly. From the original legislation—the Education of All Handicapped Children Act (EAHCA, 1975)—several reauthorizations have shifted attention from awareness of the educational issues to the meaningful participation of students with disabilities in the general classroom. The Individuals With Disabilities Education Act (IDEA, 1997) has played a major role in this evolution, with one of the most important innovations being the requirement that students with disabilities have access to the general-education curriculum. Four years after the passage of IDEA (1997), Congress passed NCLB, which shares the goal of raising expectations for the educational performance of students with disabilities and increasing accountability for their educational results. The latest reauthorization of the IDEA legislation (2004) has retained the focus on access to the general education curriculum but at the same time introduced a number of changes, several of which were intended to align IDEA with NCLB. A strengthened focus on initial instruction and accommodations within the general education curriculum ensures this alignment and access to the general education curriculum.

During these revisions, the term Response to Intervention (RtI) was explicitly incorporated into the legislation. IDEA (2004) also included three elements that integrate evidence-based practices:

1. The requirement for use of evidence-based instruction
2. Continued evaluation of student learning related to instruction
3. Emphasis on the role of data within a classroom decision-making, problem-solving approach

In addition, IDEA 2004 allows state departments and school districts to determine eligibility for learning disabilities without using the discrepancy model and IQ scores. Although not a specific focus of this book, the procedures and practices incorporated within RtI are often a significant part of revised eligibility practices for determining eligibility in various states for students with learning disabilities (Reschly & Hosp, 2004; Torgesen, 2003). Additional information related to issues of eligibility and identification of students with disabilities appears in the reference section of this book.

Previous Initiatives in Special Education

Change seems to be the only constant in education. Early legislation and research made important contributions to current legislation, and early precursors to RtI legislation and policies included special education initiatives for ensuring appropriate educational services in the least restrictive environment. Initially, the "cascade" model of special-education service delivery (Deno, 1970) described a continuum of services to meet individual student needs. This model featured steadily smaller and more intensive instructional groupings matched to a student's specific needs, resulting in a rapid increase in identification of students with a disability (specifically, learning disabilities). Several years later, Deno and Mirkin (1977) described a data-based problem-solving model for determining interventions based on observed student performance.

The Regular Education Initiative (Hallahan, Keller, McKinney, Lloyd, & Bryan, 1988) was aimed at retaining students in general education for as long as possible (McLeskey & Skiba, 1990). Soon after REI, inclusive education policies and practices (Fuchs & Fuchs, 1994) were enacted, focused on the rights and needs of students with disabilities to receive instruction in the general education setting to the greatest extent possible. Kavale and Forness (2000) suggested that the failure of both REI and inclusive education to bring about the desired changes in general and special education resulted from their emphasis on moral imperatives rather than on evidence-based practices in classroom instructional practices.

TABLE 1.1
A data-based problem-solving model for determining interventions

Problem-solving steps	Assessment Procedures	Evaluation Decisions
Problem identification	Observing and recording student performance	Does a problem exist?
Problem definition	Quantifying the perceived discrepancy	Is the problem important?
Designing intervention plans	Exploring alternative goals and solution hypotheses	What is the best solution hypothesis?
Implementing intervention	Monitoring fidelity of intervention and data collection	Is the solution attempt progressing as planned?
Problem solution	Requantifying the discrepancy	Is the original problem solved?

Adapted from *Data-based program modification: A manual,* by S. Deno & P. Mirkin, 1977, paper presented at the meeting of the Council for Exceptional Children, Reston, VA.

Most notably, educators were ill-prepared, with respect to both evidence-based instructional practices and problem-solving approaches, to meet the diverse learning needs of students in inclusive and diverse classrooms (Villa & Thousand, 1996).

Response to Intervention

Although RtI received much attention after the publication of the findings of the President's Commission on Excellence in Special Education (2002), the final rules and regulations for RtI became official only in August, 2006. Gersten and Dimino (2006) discussed the similarities between the RtI procedures and the pre-referral interventions that have been required since the 1980s for all students with special needs. The current emphasis is to direct support and professional development toward teachers implementing the interventions within the general classroom setting.

To effectively implement RtI using comprehensive, school-wide approaches, multidisciplinary teams of educators must have both an awareness of and commitment to developing and implementing instructional practices within the RtI process (Denton, 2006). The benefits of school-based, problem-solving teams include

- greater support of problem-solving solutions for teachers (Chalfant, Pysh, & Moultrie, 1979),
- increased use of interventions (Reschly & Hosp, 2004), and
- decreased referrals for special education services (Bradley, Danielson, & Doolittle, 2005).

An RtI model is a prevention model, in which the primary instruction and intervention occur in the student's current classroom as soon as problems are identified. Additional resources, interventions, and support for both the student and the teacher are also problem-solved and implemented at the classroom level (Fletcher, Denton, & Francis, 2005: Fletcher, Lyon, Fuchs, & Barnes, 2007: FDOE, 2004b; Little, 2001). Available classroom data are the primary source of information, and continued monitoring of the student's learning provides the basis for instructional decisions. Therefore, the essential components of RtI include

- an integrated data collection and assessment system to inform decisions at each tier of service delivery,
- multiple tiers of intervention service delivery, and
- a problem-solving method.

These three components encourage a different way of working to fulfill the intent of the legislators, teachers, and parents that the academic and behavioral needs for all students are met.

Integrated Data-Collection and Assessment System

An integrated data-collection and assessment system informs decisions throughout the RtI process regarding instruction and service delivery. The intent of the legislation is to create a seamless system of instruction, assessment, and service provision guided by student outcome data. To accomplish this goal, school personnel must collaborate in integrating data collection from various assessments used for both problem identification and solution monitoring (Christ, Burns, & Ysseldyke, 2005; Fuchs & Deshler, 2007; Fuchs & Fuchs, 2006a). Collaborative roles may vary with the expectations, professional experience, and settings of those involved. These school personnel—including but not limited to classroom teachers, school psychologists, reading specialists, school social workers, school counselors, occupational therapists, speech-language pathologists, and other school instructional support personnel—may be required to revise their current roles and responsibilities to meet the mandates and school district procedures associated with RtI (Dole, 2004). Position statements from the professional organizations of these school personnel were prepared and published in multiple documents, which describe the roles, responsibilities, and challenges from each perspective of the professional organization (e.g., American Speech–Language–Hearing Association, National Association of State Directors of Special Education).

Reflection Question:

- *Consider the opportunities presented by instructional problem solving and RtI. Describe the changing roles for teachers and other educators in the school.*

Given the diverse expertise of each collaborator, instructional assessment data will often contribute not only to identifying the specific problem but also to finding a solution and monitoring progress for identified student's needs. (See Appendix A for specific roles for collaborators in RtI.)

Multiple Tiers of Intervention Service Delivery

Multiple tiers of intervention service delivery assure a continuous provision of instruction and interventions to address identified student needs. The "response" component of RtI requires two specific skill applications:

- Accurate assessment of student problems
- Reliable and valid assessment of student responses to those problems at each of the multiple tiers

The "intervention" component of RtI also requires two specific skill applications:

- Interventions must be evidence-based for the type of problem, the demographics of the student (e.g., gender, race, language), and the setting factors (type of instruction, number of students in the room).
- Evidence must exist that the intervention was implemented with integrity and that the level of implementation (e.g., number of minutes per week) was documented (Fuchs et al., 2006).

Various RtI models will describe either a three- or four-tiered approach to providing services and interventions to students at increasing levels of intensity, depending on progress monitoring and data analysis (Conway & Kovalski, 1998; Jankowski, 2003; Jimerson, Burns, & VanDerHeyden, 2007; Vaughn, 2003). The rate of progress guides important educational decisions, including eligibility for support services such as reading clinics or special education (Ikeda & Gustafson, 2002). For the purposes of this book, a three-tiered model will be described (see Figure 1.1).

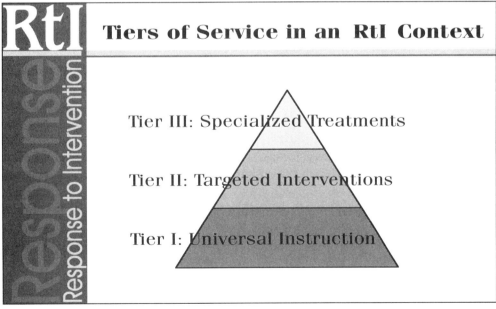

FIGURE 1.1
Three-tiered model

Tier 1: Universal Instruction (Classroom)

Instruction within classrooms is the initial focus within RtI, to determine the percentage of students responding to the "core curriculum" (both academic and behavior). Instruction during Tier 1 is generally whole-class instruction, with several important considerations. The primary characteristics of Tier 1 instruction are that

- instruction rests on evidence-based methods within the general education classroom,
- instruction using evidence-based methods includes effective teaching practices and high fidelity of implementation,
- progress monitoring occurs for all students to determine learning as a result of instruction.

NCLB (2002) presented the concept of "scientifically based instruction," which includes those methods shown in multiple research studies to result in better outcomes for students. Criteria for selection appear on the *What Works Clearinghouse* at www.w-w-c.edu. In addition, multiple research sites present reviews of research studies validating specific instructional approaches. (Please see the Resource section.) In later policies, the term "evidence-based" replaced "scientifically-based" instruction, to ensure that evidence is collected not only for initial validation during trial studies, but also after classroom implementation to ensure student outcomes have improved.

High fidelity implementation by each teacher is included in this discussion of Tier 1 instruction of the classroom curriculum. For example, implementing a content enhancement routine in a classroom relies on three critical components: cue, do, review (Lenz & Deshler, 2004). Research validating this instructional method clearly shows that each component must be implemented for improved student results. Therefore, teachers must not only teach using evidence-based instructional strategies, but also must use the instructional strategies as designed to ensure student learning.

Reflection Question:

- *As a classroom teacher, what do you believe are some of the most important components of effective teaching, especially since classroom instruction is the focus during Tier 1 of RtI?*

As an integral part of the instructional process, teachers continuously collect student performance data through observations, products, and discussions. Three questions to consider when evaluating the rates and types of learning for all of the students include the following:

- Is the core curriculum effective? That is, do 80% of students meet the established benchmarks?
- Which students are at risk for failure?
- Does any over-representation of particular student groups appear in those students identified as at risk?

If this instruction is adequately differentiated, 80 to 90% of the students will achieve established benchmarks of the curriculum. Assessments occur three to four times per year. The following points summarize Tier 1 of RtI related to universal, interventions within classrooms:

- Assess students continuously. Measure *all* student progress against grade-level progress. Look at progress of all subgroups (AYP categories).
- Begin with whole-class intervention strategies.
- Differentiate instruction as needed.
- Monitor and assess student progress using authentic, same-day result-oriented measures.
- Measure and monitor all student progress in classroom.

Tier 2: Targeted Interventions

If students do not make adequate progress in Tier 1, more intensive services and targeted interventions, usually in small-group settings, are provided in addition to instruction in the general curriculum. Progress is monitored more closely, at least bi-weekly, and research-based interventions could last approximately 6 to 10 weeks. Tier 2 interventions have the following primary characteristics:

- Interventions are delivered to smaller groups of students, either within or outside the general-education classroom.
- Interventions are provided *in addition to* core instruction.
- Interventions focus on particular skill areas that need strengthening.

Targeted interventions may include specialized services from a literacy teacher, additional resources such as a more intensive reading program, participating in a small group of students during direct instruction, or additional time. Estimates are that 5 to 10% of the students may need targeted interventions to meet the grade-level benchmarks. Often the same measures as in Tier 1 are used to monitor progress of student performance and assess performance. A small percentage of students will not respond to Tier 2 levels of instruction and will require the most intensive instruction (Tier 3). The following points summarize Tier 2 of RtI as target interventions within classrooms for students not responding to differentiated instruction from Tier 1:

- Students are those in general education classrooms who have not met curricular benchmarks through whole class interventions
- Interventions do not replace classroom instruction, but work in a mutual dependence relationship to expand classroom lessons.
- Interventions are conducted by a specialist or teacher with groups of five or fewer students.
- Interventions are intense (an additional 30 minutes of instruction per day), and student responses are closely monitored and documented and are designed to produce immediate results.
- Research-based resources are identified and implemented to meet the needs of identified students.

Tier 3: Specialized, Intensive Intervention

Students who continue to fall short of the grade-level benchmarks after differentiated, explicit instruction of the core curriculum in the classroom (Tier 1) and more intensive, targeted instruction (Tier 2) may be eligible for special education services under the Individuals with Disabilities Education Act (IDEA, 2004). During Tier 3, interventions are based on individual student needs and use diagnostic assessment to inform intervention development. Additional testing may be warranted, and students receive individualized, intensive interventions targeted to the skills deficits. Progress monitoring of intervention effectiveness is the same for Tier 3 as in Tier 2. Only 1 to 5% of students would be considered for the intensive interventions and possible referrals for specialized services of Tier 3. Characteristics of Tier 3 interventions are the following:

- Interventions are delivered to very small groups of students or to students individually.
- Interventions are provided *in addition to* Tier 1 instruction. Tier 3 interventions should include the most instructional minutes. It is critical that Tier 3 instruction *does not supplant* or replace the core instruction.
- Interventions focus more narrowly on defined skill areas.

Tier 3 is the most intense level of intervention provided to students in general education. A student who does not respond to Tier 3 interventions may qualify for special education services when the intensity or type of intervention required to improve student performance exceeds the resources in general education or is unavailable in general education settings. Tier 3's intensive intervention may include special education services, reading services, or other program options, as necessary and appropriate. The following points summarize Tier 3's intensive, specialized interventions:

- Students are those in general-education classrooms who have not met curricular benchmarks through whole-class and selected interventions.
- A specialist works with small groups of two or three students or provides one-on-one tutoring.
- Interventions are in addition to the teaching time and curriculum offered with Tiers 1 and 2 intervention.
- Continued intensive instruction is provided while student progress and the instructional program are monitored.

The tiers of instruction and intervention vary in minutes of instruction, resources, number of students in the group, frequency of assessment, and focus of instruction, ranging from a broad focus in Tier 1 to a very narrow focus in Tier 3. Each school may have very different tiers depending on the needs of its students, but the underlying principles of time, size of group, assessment, and focus should remain consistent across schools.

A Problem-Solving Method

Implementation of RtI depends on educators' use of a problem-solving method throughout a school through a systematic approach to address students' academic and behavior needs in relation to the curriculum goals. The process of instructional problem solving includes the following steps:

1. Reviewing the student's strengths and weaknesses
2. Identifying instructional interventions
3. Collecting student progress data
4. Evaluating the effectiveness of the interventions

A problem-solving approach is consistent with federal and state mandates and policies and it also provides instructionally relevant information in a timely manner to teachers and educators. The problem-solving process is cyclical; it identifies classroom concerns by using assessment information, developing a plan from alternatives, and implementing and monitoring the effect on student achievement. Models described for problem solving have similar components, and Table 1.2 shows a comparison of the problem-solving models from three different sources. Although the components are slightly different, the components and process are similar.

When considering the components of problem solving, educators can rely on their experience with multiple components of both the process of problem solving and RtI procedures. For example, teachers routinely use the results of curriculum-based classroom assessments to adjust teaching and curriculum in their classrooms and to provide specific feedback and adjustments to individual students. Additionally, student results have been reported both to individuals (e.g., grade cards, IEPs) and to groups (e.g., reports to administrators and school boards) for years. With the legislation of RtI, however, high-quality teaching and assessment methods are systematically collected, reviewed, and presented to ensure student progress, especially for students who are not successful in school.

NCLB mandates disaggregating student data into subpopulations to determine the Annual Yearly Progress (AYP) achievement for each of the groups of students (ESE, ESOL, etc.). Through disaggregation of the data by the specific student groups, information about the achievement of specific groups of students becomes available. A comprehensive, school-wide RtI process, using teams of educational professionals, will serve as the problem-solving system for data collection, problem solving, action planning, and continuous progress monitoring.

TABLE 1.2
A comparison of the problem-solving models from three different sources

Problem-Solving Process (Deno & Mirkin, 1977)	IDEAL Problem-Solving Model (Bransford & Stein, 1984)	Action Research Process (FDOE, 2004b)
Problem identification	Identify the problem	Identify and define the problem
Problem definition	Define the problem	
Designing intervention plans	Explore alternative solutions	Develop and implement action plan
Implementing intervention	Apply the chosen solution	Collect and analyze data
Problem solution	Look at the effects	Use and share the results

The characteristics of RtI may be summarized as follows:

- Universal screening of *all* students through effective, research-based instructional methods and resources
- Use of the problem-solving process to address classroom and school-wide concerns
- Measurement of student responses to interventions using assessment data
- Use of student RtI data to change the intensity or form of new interventions within a school-wide, comprehensive system of instruction and intervention.

Summary

Response to Intervention is a comprehensive, data-based system for identifying, defining, and resolving students' academic and behavioral difficulties in schools. Response to Intervention, in many ways, is another term for "data-based decision making" applied to education. It is a collaborative, integrated process focused on implementing high-quality, evidence-based practices, based on identified, individual student needs. These data-based, problem-solving approaches are applied at the classroom, school, and district levels to address the academic and behavioral needs of students.

RtI has two overarching goals: to deliver evidence-based instruction and interventions to improve student learning and to collect information regarding students' response to those interventions, to be used as a basis for continued interventions or program placements. While special-education eligibility decisions can be a product of these efforts, they are not the primary goal.

RtI procedures provide the framework for making decisions about student instruction, interventions, and program placements, as indicated by continuous progress monitoring. Special-education services in terms of what each student needs are determined by the student's rate of response to intervention and the size of the gap between the student and the benchmark. As a result, identification is not about the student's label, but rather about determining what interventions are most helpful in closing the gap in a timely manner.

Special education services can be a means of providing specific, effective intervention services for students, and they are inherently linked to instructional efforts that occurred in general education. The delivery of special education programs is not linear, where special-education programs are the last thing on the line (and sometimes a goal, or end in itself). Rather, special education programs are part of an integrated service delivery system.

Reflective Questions:

- *What does this legislation about RtI mean to me?*
- *How will RtI affect my current and evolving role within my school?*
- *Why is RtI important to me? To my students? To my school district?*
- *How will collaboration with other professionals assist me in meeting these goals?*

CHAPTER 2

WHAT? An Overview of Classroom Instructional Problem Solving

Overview

This chapter provides brief overviews and descriptions of classroom instructional problem solving and action research, including the characteristics of ethical commitment, a cycle of reflective practice, and collaboration. Reflective questions and examples engage the reader with these processes and evoke consideration of educators' professional needs and responsibilities with respect to instructional problem solving. Theoretical models align the problem-solving process with the RtI process.

Reflection Questions:

- *What is action research and classroom instructional problem solving?*
- *When will I use this process in my current role in my school?*
- *How will this process help me with my current responsibilities in my school?*
- *How is this process related to RtI?*

"You can either take action, or you can hang back and hope for a miracle. Miracles are great, but they are so unpredictable."

~Peter Drucker

A major emphasis on reform of education continues, with change seemingly the only constant. Change requires awareness of classroom concerns, an action plan, and continued support. Purposeful change in the teaching and learning process requires teachers and students to be involved in the decisions that directly affect that process. As educators engage in action research related to classroom instructional problem solving, they become agents of change. Teachers are consciously planning for changes in their classroom and using data to plan and to monitor students' learning.

As mentioned in chapter 1, the characteristics and processes of both action research and classroom instructional problem solving have a rich tradition in educational research and theory. Both exhibit three major characteristics: ethical commitment, a cycle of reflective practice, and collaboration.

Ethical commitment to professional practices to assure continued learning for all students is the foundation of this educational process for any teacher. Teachers and school educators must be willing to ask and search for answers to questions such as the following:

- How can I best serve the students that I teach?
- Whose needs are not being met?
- What can I do to improve my practice for all students?

A teacher with ethical commitment is motivated by a concern for the equity of opportunity for all students. In addition to complying with mandates and policies, as part of the ethical commitment to educate all students each teacher and member of classroom and school-based problem-solving teams must be willing to answer these critical questions about instructional practices. Calhoun (2002) provided useful guidelines for school-based problem-solving teams:

- Relationships are equal, not hierarchal. Leadership shifts and depends on expertise and the challenge at hand, rather than on position.
- Communication is authentic, sincere, and open.
- Participation is focused, active, and supportive of goals and directions.

The goal of classroom instructional problem solving (action research) is to improve instruction, and it is practiced by a person or group of people who want to improve student results. Therefore, classroom teachers and other school-based educators create and follow the plan (design), collect information (data), analyze the information, and summarize the findings. These activities form a continuous cycle of reflective practice of instructional and program improvement to meet the goals of academic and behavioral mastery for the students.

As noted in the previous chapter, while the specific titles of the steps or phases of instructional problem solving or action research may vary, the process is similar. Teachers and school-based educators identify instructional (content or behavioral) concerns when reviewing assessment information (data) and collaboratively develop an action plan for instruction or intervention. Monitoring the results of the action plan in terms of student results provides additional information. These activities continue throughout each of the RtI tiers to ensure increased intensity of interventions within classrooms prior to determining eligibility for other programs, such as special-education programs. Figure 2.1 shows this cycle of continuous problem solving.

Collaboration by the members of the RtI team enhances problem solving. Promoted by the medical, organizational, and mental health professions,

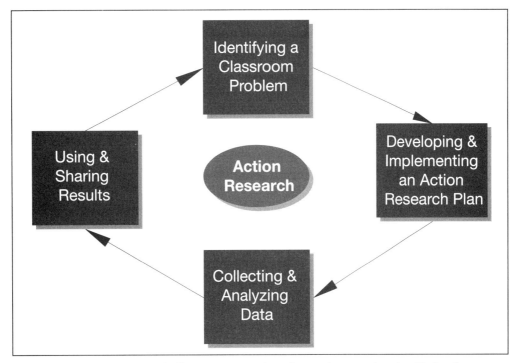

From *Summative report of effective instructional-practices project* (p. 5), by the Florida Department of Education, 2004, Tallahassee, FL: Author. Copyright 2004 by the Florida Department of Education. Reprinted with permission.

FIGURE 2.1
Cycle of instructional problem solving (action research).

collaboration is defined similarly in the three contexts, and the goal of collaboration within schools is to solve a current problem involving students and to help the education professionals solve similar problems in the future (Deno, 1970). An early definition of collaboration provided by Idol, Paolucci-Whitcomb, and Nevin (1986, p. 1) continues to be used in special education:

> Collaborative consultation is an interactive process that enables teams of people with diverse expertise to generate creative solutions to mutually defined problems. The outcome is enhanced, altered, and produces solutions that are different from those that the individual team member would produce independently.

The resulting collaborative partnerships enhance the process of problem solving by invoking the leadership and expertise from each of the team members (Fullan, 2005).

The purposes of collaborative instructional problem-solving teams are to

- brainstorm further solutions to successfully meet the needs of students in classrooms and schools,
- empower school staff and classroom teachers with the skills and processes to solve academic or behavioral classroom problems, and
- support teachers when considering multiple options to solving classroom problems.

As mentioned above, communication skills are very important within a collaborative relationship. Several of the resources listed in this text provide more complete information on the topics of collaboration and communication.

As school staff and classroom teachers are finding solutions, support and empowerment are critical to their success within the RtI process. During any of the RtI tiers, school personnel may want to complete the reflection activity in Appendix B, which reviews several of the key components for creating a comprehensive problem-solving team within the school. As mentioned, instructional problem solving and action research refer to the continuous process of finding solutions. The term "action research," already familiar to many teachers and school-based educators, is briefly described in the next section.

Definition of Action Research

Action research is a form of professional development in which educators study student learning related to their own teaching, a process that allows them to learn about their own practice. Schmuck (1997) compares action research to looking into a mirror at oneself taking action. Conducting action research provides educators with an avenue to reflect on their own teaching practices and to engage in self-directed learning with the ultimate goal of improving student learning. For students to reach optimal learning, teachers must continuously build upon their own knowledge of student learning and intentionally study their own practices as they are being implemented in the classroom.

The National Staff Development Council created standards for staff development (NSDC, 2000) that emphasize that professional development must be results-driven, standards-based, and job-embedded. Effective professional development affects student learning, and action research is one form of professional development that is results-driven, standards-based, and job-embedded (Hirsch, 2004). Educators might consider the following specific questions, which reflect practices that teachers use when they conduct action research:

- Do you purposefully observe and assess your students to determine areas of change?
- Do you design instructional plans to bring about the change?
- Do you continuously monitor your instruction to ensure that the change has occurred to affect student learning?

A number of researchers have commented on the importance of action research. Glanz (2003) refers to action research as "disciplined inquiry." When educators conduct action research, they are deliberate about the data they collect, the decisions they make, and the lessons they teach. Hubbard and Power (1999, p. 23) note that "action research is a natural extension of good teaching. Observing students closely, analyzing their needs, and adjusting the curriculum to fit the needs of all students have always been important skills demonstrated by fine teachers." Calhoun (2002) observes that when educators conduct action research, they ask themselves a critical question, "Am I making an impact on student learning?" When teachers notice a breakdown in learning, they systematically and intentionally plan instruction to meet the needs of their students.

The primary goal of action research is to improve student learning by developing and refining the skill of teaching. Pursuing this goal is empowering for teachers, giving them opportunities to grow within their professional role and responsibilities (Henson, 1996; Little & Houston, 2003).

Action research is a continuous, reflective process whereby educators make instructional decisions in their classrooms based on the student needs reflected in classroom data. Four phases characterize action research (Little, 2003):

1. Identifying a classroom problem
2. Developing and implementing an action research plan
3. Collecting and analyzing data
4. Using and sharing results

Because learning is a cyclical process, action research never really ends. An action researcher is always observing, analyzing, designing, assessing, and adjusting. The cyclical nature of action research provides teachers with ongoing opportunities to reflect on and refine their own teaching practices (FDOE, 2004b).

Connections: Action Research and Instructional Problem Solving with RtI

RtI is a systematic, data-based method for identifying, defining, and resolving students' academic or behavioral difficulties relying on a collaborative, school-wide, problem-solving approach. As a proactive and prevention-focused approach, RtI encourages teams of educators to develop dynamic instructional plans to address academic or behavioral concerns of individual students, initially within the general-education classroom. RtI uses and adapts evidence-based instructional approaches, resources, and strategies within the classroom, while continuously monitoring student learning that results from the teacher's varied instructional methods.

Classroom teachers are the primary participants in the RtI process, but other educators (e.g., reading teacher, speech–language pathologist, school psychologist) may participate on the school-based team to contribute to both the identification of and the possible solutions for instructional concerns of identified students. The connections between classroom instructional problem solving and the RtI process, therefore, exhibit numerous similarities and subtle differences.

Reflection Questions

- *Why should you conduct classroom instructional problem solving?*
- *What are the benefits of classroom instructional problem solving to teachers and students?*
- *How could participating in this process affect your professional practice?*
- *Do you have concerns about conducting this process in your classroom or school?*

Benefits of Problem Solving

Classroom instructional problem solving within the RtI framework provides many benefits to students, teachers, and schools.

TABLE 2.1
Comparison of problem-solving (action research) and RtI

Problem-Solving (Action Research)	Characteristic	Response to Intervention
Process, data-based approach to classroom instructional concerns	Approach	Framework of data-based, school-wide instruction and interventions
To improve student achievement through teacher inquiry	Goal	To improve student achievement through high-fidelity implementation of evidence-based instruction
Cyclical	Format	Cyclical through 3 or 4 described tiers
Teachers	Members	Teams of teachers, school psychologists, speech-language pathologists, reading coaches, social workers, and other school personnel, as appropriate
3 types: individual, collaborative, school	Application	School-based, problem-solving team
Student achievement, teacher professional development, endorsement, certification	Major uses	Student achievement, student pre-referral and eligibility for special education, if appropriate
Professional development	Impetus	Legislation
Collaboration, trust, communication, problem-solving, organization	Skills needed	Collaboration, trust, communication, problem-solving, organization
Time for collaboration, knowledge of and access to evidenced-based instructional strategies and assessment, knowledge of problem-solving process, administrative support, and skilled colleagues	Resources needed	Time for collaboration, knowledge of and access to evidenced-based instructional strategies and assessment, knowledge of problem-solving process, administrative support, and skilled colleagues

Student Benefits

Students benefit because their learning is being studied and instructional practices are designed to accelerate learning and build on student knowledge. Close monitoring throughout the process ensures that appropriate progress is being made and, if it is not, adjustments in instruction will occur.

Teacher Benefits

Teachers benefit because the process allows them to think about, study, and refine their own professional practice. By participating, the teacher develops a sense of ownership in the knowledge constructed, and this sense of ownership fosters real change in the classroom (Dana & Yendol-Silva, 2003).

The educator's main goal in professional development and classroom implementation of evidence-based instructional practices and knowledge is to increase student learning. Implementing findings can convert professional development into actual classroom practice, while focusing on the impact on student learning as a result. In addition, this process encourages collaboration at many different levels and among educators with diverse expertise, which can counteract the common feeling of isolation among teachers.

School Benefits

Schools benefit because the goal is improving student achievement. When teachers are engaged and the process is well supported, a learning community can develop, encouraging professional dialogue, learning, and research, affecting all students. As more schools implement procedures as part of comprehensive RtI initiatives within schools and school districts, action research will enjoy increased attention as part of classroom instructional problem solving.

Summary

Classroom instructional problem solving and action research encourage teachers to inquire into instructional issues and concerns within their classrooms in a cycle of instruction and reflection. Educators use this method to identify the problem, design the plan, collect continuous student data, monitor the instructional plan, analyze the data of student results, and summarize the findings. Through a team approach to the three tiers of instruction and intervention (universal, targeted, and specialized), it puts into practice the newly mandated RtI process, in which student data provide the catalyst for instruction and intervention in both academic and behavioral concerns of identified students.

The next chapter will discuss initiation of classroom instructional problem-solving practices and procedures in schools as part of the RtI initiative.

Reflection Questions:

- *Define the terms action research and classroom instructional problem solving.*
- *Describe the process of action research.*
- *List and describe the three approaches of action research.*
- *Provide benefits of this process for the student, teacher, and school.*
- *Thinking about your classroom and students, how can engaging in this process benefit you as a teacher as well as your students?*
- *Describe the differences and similarities of action research and classroom instructional problem solving with the process of Response to Intervention.*

CHAPTER 3

WHERE and WHEN? Classroom Questions in My Classroom Now

Overview

This chapter describes the structure of a comprehensive system for implementing Response to Intervention in schools. Reflective questions, examples, and checklists encourage readers to consider the current demands regarding student achievement made in their state, school district, school, and classroom. The material in this chapter enables readers to identify their current instructional questions and align them with the curricular and instructional expectations for the special-education process. Problem solving within classrooms under the mandated RtI process constitutes an initial step of determining eligibility for special education.

Reflection Questions:

- *What are the key components for an RtI problem-solving team in schools?*
- *What are several considerations, differences, and procedures related to the RtI process?*
- *How do all educators become engaged in this RtI problem-solving process?*

"Never doubt that a small group of thoughtful committed people can change the world: indeed it is the only thing that ever has."
~ Margaret Mead

Increasingly, educators recognize that the academic and behavioral needs of students who are at risk can best be met if professionals work together as collaborative teams in designing and delivering educational programs. The learning and behavioral concerns regarding some students may be complex, requiring the expertise of more than one professional. Collaboration to address student concerns can occur in multiple ways, such as

- coteaching a diverse group of students;
- codeveloping a behavior intervention plan or an individual education plan;
- coaching to enhance various instructional methods;
- creating grade-level or subject teams of experts; and
- creating student success teams, prereferral teams, and academic success teams.

Regardless of the type and purpose of the team, meaningful communication and collaboration among team members enhance the productivity and outcomes of the team. The most effective teams are those in which the professionals pool their expertise to create solutions to the stated problems. Although communication is not a specific focus of this book, individual team members should possess and exhibit effective communication and team-building skills.

Reflection Questions:

Consider the most highly effective team that you have been a member, including sports, personal, or professional.

- *Why did you select that team?*
- *What characteristics made that team effective?*
- *Have you been on an educational team that you felt was highly effective?*
- *How can educational teams be highly effective? What is needed to assure this high quality?*

As educators within classrooms, schools, and school districts continue to implement RtI, new procedures, policies, and practices will be developed to meet its mandate. As part of this compliance, educators will serve collaboratively on comprehensive, multidisciplinary RtI teams which have the responsibilities, skills, and tasks needed to meet the overall mission of the team: to use problem solving to create an instructional or intervention plan based on individual learner needs. (Appendix A lists the usual membership on the RtI team.) Although the RtI model seems simple and straightforward, putting its process into action requires much consideration and planning to make it valid, reliable, and feasible (Bender & Shores, 2007).

Two Models of RtI

In early research, two implementation models emerged for RtI—the problem-solving model and the standard protocol model. The problem-solving model focuses on individualized classroom decision-making about instruction and intervention for each student, whereas the standard protocol model rests on a set of standard research-based interventions.

Problem-Solving Model

The problem-solving model is presently defined as "a process that includes an objective definition of student behavior problems or academic difficulties, systematic analysis of the student's problem and implementation of a planned systematic set of interventions" (Grimes & Kurns, 2003, pg. 3). This definition evolved through research over a number of years.

Bergan (1977) and Deno and Mirkin (1977) approached RtI through problem solving. In his research, on student issues, Bergan (1977) employed a model consisting of specific steps to

- define the problem,
- determine the performance gap between current functioning and expected behavior, and
- develop an intervention and data-collection assessments based on scientifically validated practices.

After these steps were completed, the student data collected led to programming decisions on behalf of the student. The team-based "problem-solving approach" evolved from Bergan's basic design.

Another problem-solving model, developed by the Heartland Area Educational Agency in Iowa, involved instruction and assessment at the student level (Tilly, 2003). Heartland incorporated the "science into practice" concept by applying the scientific model to the classroom decision-making process. Research using this model reports a significant reduction in special-education placement rates for students in kindergarten through grade 3 (Tilly, 2003).

Numerous school districts have refined and replicated the model, including the Minneapolis Public Schools and the Heartland Area Consortium in Iowa. These problem-solving procedures are sequenced into a more formal pattern of stages or tiers, leading from classroom instruction to possible referral for consideration for special services, including special education. For example, in Minneapolis, the sequential stages include the following (Marston, Muyskens, Lau, & Canter, 2003):

- Stage 1: Classroom interventions
- Stage 2: Problem-solving team interventions
- Stage 3: Special-education referral and initiation of due process procedures.

Standard Protocol Model

The standard protocol model uses a set of standard research-based interventions usually implemented in each tier of instruction and intervention. These interventions and instructional approaches are employed with various levels of intensity in terms of time, numbers of students, and so on, depending on the student's instructional needs.

For example, research conducted in elementary schools in Nashville (McMaster, Fuchs, Fuchs, & Compton, 2003) and New York (Vellutino, Scanlon, Small, & Fanuele, 2006) indicated significant improvements in reading with early elementary students. When students were identified as at risk in early reading skills, classroom teachers used one of two research-based strategies during the first tier of instruction. In addition, students received ongoing progress monitoring through nonword fluency probes from the Dynamic Indicators of Basic Early Literacy Skills, or DIBELS (Good & Kaminski, 2002). In research-based strategies, data from the DIBELS continuous progress monitoring probes identified students as responders and non-responders at the first tier of classroom instruction. Non-responding students received additional, more intensive instruction and intervention. In both research settings, initial results indicated a significant improvement in reading ability for the identified students.

The two RtI models exhibit a number of notable similarities and important subtle differences. Table 3.1 compares the attributes of both RtI models as described in the research.

Although educators need to be aware of the components of the researched RtI models, this book focuses on the procedures, practices, and considerations necessary for problem solving under either RtI model. This chapter describes specific considerations for initially establishing an RtI team within a school. The next chapter looks at both the content of evidence-based instruction and the process of problem-solving that serves to put the RtI process and procedures into practice in schools under both RtI models.

Getting Started With RtI Teams

Members of the multidisciplinary school-wide RtI team meet to problem-solve educational concerns presented by members of the team. Chapter 1 and

TABLE 3.1
Comparison of Two Models of Response to Intervention (RtI) *

Problem-Solving Model**	Standard Protocol Model
Decisions based on individual student needs	Clear, scientific process in literature for strategies and assessment
Allows more flexibility in choices of interventions and allocations of resources	Standard interventions in place and readily available for students in need
	Structured progression among tiers
May be more time-consuming as problems are solved at the individual student level	Less flexibility with choice of interventions.
Requires teachers and team members to have vast knowledge and expertise in research-based strategies	May require additional staff, depending on available resources

* Adapted from *Response to intervention: A practical guide for every teacher* (p. 15), by W. N. Bender and C. Shores, 2007, Thousand Oaks, CA: Corwin Press. Copyright by Corwin Press. Reprinted with permission.
** The RtI model is named the "Problem-Solving Model" but should not be confused with the process of problem-solving. See additional information in the text regarding both the model and the process of problem-solving.

Appendix A suggest the educational professionals who may be team members, and additional members may be requested to participate as indicated by the needs of students who will be discussed at a given RtI meeting (e.g., the school nurse if a health issue is suspected). The presence of teachers is critical to the team meeting, especially that of the referring teacher who has requested assistance and ideas from the RtI team.

Clearly defined membership, roles, responsibilities, and procedures are essential to the RtI team's effectiveness. During the organizational period, input from district and school leadership personnel can shape the focus, expectations, responsibilities, and requirements for the team's functioning, resulting in a common framework for the important work of the individual members of the team. Clarity leads to effective team functioning and use of the team by the faculty within the school.

Team Membership

The RtI team's first decisions relate to membership and roles within the team. Active involvement of school administrators on the team produces administrative support and awareness of RtI. Educators with diverse expertise in content, assessment, instructional pedagogy, and instructional interventions, as well as coaching and facilitation, should be considered for membership on the team. In deciding on membership, the team may want to use the questions provided in Appendix B, and in deciding on length of service, the team should recognize that members who continue to serve on the team for a period of time provide stability of team processes.

Decisions regarding meeting times, locations, and meeting procedures, as well as the identity of the RtI team facilitator and team recorder, are important to convey to the school's faculty. The form in Appendix C provides a sample RtI organization chart to assist with these initial procedures.

Initial meetings will continue to clarify the purpose, expectations, and responsibilities for the team members, not only with the team but also within the faculty school community, especially with respect to strengths, resources, and personnel that will contribute to the RtI team functioning. Specific issues to consider include the following:

- How do educators in the school currently support students and their teachers when considering additional supports and interventions? What procedures can be enhanced or revised within an RtI system?
- What sources of assessment data are continuously collected, aggregated, and available for school staff, especially faculty?
- What resources are available to teachers and educational personnel (e.g., reading coaches and interventionists) to differentiate instruction or provide various interventions for students? Are these resources research-based?
- What opportunities currently exist for teams of educators to meet and discuss instructional issues and concerns? Is time for collaboration built into the school schedule?
- What is the current knowledge about RtI among faculty and staff in the school?
- Is professional development provided, both initially and on-going, through high-quality implementation and interventions within classrooms?

Discussions and decisions about these important organizational considerations will affect the functioning of the RtI team. (See Appendix D for an example of an RtI implementation planning form.) These discussions should be held at the very outset of beginning the RtI initiative within the school, and once decisions are made, RtI team members should communicate the processes and procedures to faculty within the school.

Effective Team Functioning

Clarity regarding team roles, processes, and procedures provides a common framework for the important work of the individual members of this committee. Clarity also results in effective team functioning, and awareness and use by the faculty within the school. Effectiveness results from the following considerations:

- Does a meeting format exist, and is it followed?
- Have the team facilitator and recorder guided the overall team functioning?
- Was the meeting time used effectively?
- Were the RtI members supportive of each other and the referring teacher?
- Was specific and adequate assessment and instruction information provided?
- Were the instructional and intervention plans and resources available to the classroom teacher?
- Was a clearly defined implementation and follow-up plan written?
- How will integrity of implementation (both classroom instruction and RtI action plan) be supported and monitored?

With each referral and team meeting, members of the RtI team should debrief and reflect on the overall functioning and resulting plans determined at the meeting. An RtI team discussion form is included in Appendix E. Consideration of the RtI team members' needs for resources, professional development, and answers to specific questions is very important during the initial stages of the RtI team development process since the team members are often approached by other faculty and staff with informational questions during the early days of RtI implementation.

The need for support may arise in diverse areas. For example, if a member of the team has concerns regarding the skills and format to use when problem solving, professional development on this process may be important for all members of the team to ensure high-quality functioning during RtI meetings. In addition, classroom teachers must receive the necessary support and professional development regarding research-based instruction and interventions. Suggested topics for professional development include the following:

- Active engagement strategies to improve student academic learning time
- Instructional approaches (direct instruction, precision teaching, coteaching, reciprocal teaching, class-wide peer tutoring, etc.)
- Metacognitive and cognitive strategy instruction
- Classroom and behavior management (motivation, classroom procedures, behavioral contracting, reinforcement strategies, self-management, etc.)

- Formal and informal assessments (curriculum-based, rubrics, etc.)
- Instructional accommodations and modifications
- Explanation of the process of problem solving, including review of necessary communication skills

Awareness of the Team and Use by the Faculty

Knowledge and skills relating to the problem-solving process and research-based methods improve the functioning and results of the RtI teams. Once the responsibilities of the team and its procedures have been determined, and after any professional development needed for the RtI team has been completed, the team's next goal is to cultivate awareness and use of the RtI process for classroom instructional problem-solving within the school.

To reach all target audiences, members of the RtI team must disseminate awareness information to the faculty and staff in multiple formats (e.g., staff newsletters, faculty meetings, team meetings, brochures for parents and faculty, etc.). These multiple approaches are especially important at the outset of the RtI initiative, as many questions will arise about the new team. Informational resources and websites from numerous professional educational agencies and regional resource centers may prove valuable in addressing the questions and concerns of faculty, staff, and parents. (See the Resource section in the Appendix for suggestions of various resources and websites.)

Usually, classroom teachers will initiate the RtI process, and therefore they need access not only to the process but to the necessary referral forms. These forms must request sufficient background information for the team members to understand the teacher's expectations and specific concerns regarding the student. Also, the forms and processes should encourage teachers to pursue continued assistance. (Appendix F shows an example of a teacher referral form).

Initially, teachers may want a member of the RtI team to assist with the process to request assistance from the members of the RtI team. Once the completed form has been submitted to a team member (usually the RtI facilitator), it may be helpful to meet with the teacher before the RtI meeting is scheduled to clarify and expand the form's information. In addition, members of the team may want to review or collect additional information related to the instructional concerns. For example, if the teacher is concerned that a student is not progressing in early literacy (e.g., learning the initial phonemes), the reading coach may review the most current DIBELS scores and other curriculum-based assessment information routinely given to the students in the school.

As soon as possible, an RtI team meeting with the concerned teacher should be scheduled at a mutually agreed upon time and location. Each member of the team should bring any pertinent information to the meeting, as the goal of this meeting is to develop an instructional plan to address the described concerns. In addition, follow-up plans, including assessments for continuous progress monitoring, will be developed at this meeting. This process may occur when problem-solving instructional concerns arise in Tiers 1, 2, or 3, and the intensity of interventions will continue to increase for students who do not respond to previous instructional or intervention plans developed by the RtI committee during the problem-solving process.

Summary

Problem solving drives the implementation of RtI in schools. Guidelines for successful RtI problem solving within a school include the following (adapted from Lau, Sieler, Muyskens, Canter, VanKeuren, & Marston, 2006):

- Establish an RtI team that includes general-education teachers as well as other educators with diverse expertise.
- Develop and prepare an implementation manual detailing procedures, expectations, specific forms, and time frames for each tier and step of the process.
- Provide in-depth professional development (awareness, coaching, and mentoring) to assist teachers and other educators in understanding and implementing the RtI process.
- Communicate with and encourage participation by key stakeholders (teachers, parents, administrators, and community members).
- Provide time for planning, professional development, meetings, and ongoing monitoring and evaluation.
- Consider developing school-wide interventions that use current resources (e.g., school-wide after-school tutoring programs).

In the next chapter, the classroom instructional problem-solving process will be described in detail, including the mention of resources and examples of helpful forms.

CHAPTER 4

HOW? The Four Phases of Classroom Instructional Problem Solving

Overview

This chapter is presented in four sections to clearly show how instructional problem solving is a cyclical and continuous process within the RtI framework. This initial section will briefly highlight the process, and an anticipation guide (Appendix G) will foster further understanding.

"A (classroom) problem adequately stated is a (classroom) problem well on its way to being solved."

~R. Buckminster Fuller

Reflection Questions:

- *How do I describe questions for investigating classroom concerns?*
- *How do I identify a classroom problem through reflection and initial data collection and analysis?*
- *How do I create a problem statement related to current classroom data and the expectations for learning for students in my classroom?*

Meeting the learning needs of all students in a class can be a daunting task. Given the diverse learning needs of the students and the many demands on teachers' time (including some that are not related directly to teaching), even finding time to learn about the students and their backgrounds, skills, and abilities can be difficult. The bottom line for each teacher, however, must be, "Are all of my students learning?" To answer this question accurately, teachers must continuously observe, think about, and analyze student learning relative to mastery of grade-level curricular standards and expectations. The classroom instructional problem-solving process provides the means for educators to become more efficient and effective in their examination of student learning because it identifies specific instructional needs based on student data. Basing instructional decisions on classroom data leads to instruction that is designed to target the identified strengths and needs of the students. A period of analysis and reflection provides the information needed to identify classroom instructional concerns.

Reflection Questions:

* *Consider the actions of medical doctors when they are preparing to treat patients.*
* *What planning and preparations are completed by doctors while diagnosing concerns and problems of their patients?*
* *How are the actions of teachers similar to doctors when considering classroom instructional concerns?*

Before doctors treat a patient, they must first learn as much as possible about the patient's concerns and identify the source of the problem areas to address, a question to be answered, or a phenomenon to be explained. At times, the doctors must review previous records, meet with and interview the patient and family members, prescribe additional diagnostic assessments, and often collaborate with other health and medical professionals to accurately diagnose the problem and prescribe appropriate medical treatments for the patient. Once a medical plan is prescribed, follow-up appointments, further assessments, and referrals for specialized treatments are often needed.

When using the RtI process, teachers must begin by identifying an issue of concern in the classroom, such as a need that is reflected in a level of student learning that falls below academic or behavioral expectations. To adequately identify a problem, a teacher must take the time to investigate areas of concern by collecting and analyzing information about the students' learning needs related to the curriculum expectations of the grade level. "Teachers who rush to complete the problem formulation stage are more likely to flounder in their later efforts, whereas teachers who take their time to reflect on and define their problem are more likely to pursue questions yielding meaningful results" (Sagor, 2005, p. 32). Problem formulation can be completed individually, in teams, or collaboratively within the school, as well as within the context of the instructional problem-solving RtI team meetings. Using the anticipation guide included in Appendix G can help in considering the instructional problem-solving process.

Reflection Questions:

- *Why is my role as a classroom teacher so important to the RtI process?*
- *What actions of teachers are related to instructional problem solving?*
- *Why is this process of classroom instructional problem solving important for the students in the classroom and school?*

Phase 1: Investigating and Identifying a Problem

In the first phase, the most difficult phase of the process, the guiding questions for investigating classroom concerns are named and described. Multiple samples, checklists, and guiding questions can help pinpoint a concern or issue on which to focus, either with a small group of students, an individual student, or an entire classroom. This section describes the components of the problem statement and provides multiple examples. In addition, the forms and case studies included in the Appendix will help in completing not only this first phase but also the remaining three phases of instructional problem solving.

"A problem is the discrepancy between unsatisfactory present situations and more desirable goals."
~Richard Schmuck

To begin investigating classroom concerns, teachers must first observe, question, and reflect on the entire classroom or a group of students. Evaluating the current situation and comparing it to the expectations, curricular standards, and benchmarks for all students will produce data and information regarding the instructional concern or issue to study. Since curricular standards determine academic goals for the students, they must be considered in the formative stages of this problem-solving process. Figure 4.1 provides an example of an informal rubric aligned with the curricular standards in the content of language (including reading, speaking, and listening). As an informal assessment instrument based on the curriculum standards, it can be used to collect initial individual performance or achievement information. Observing and interviewing students while they are engaged in learning, analyzing their work samples, and collecting classroom assessments can be time-consuming, yet necessary at this phase. Collaboration with another teacher, mentor, or instructional coach can be helpful, especially if this person has observed the students in the class.

Several considerations and questions can assist the classroom teacher in observing, collecting informal assessment information, and reflecting on the strengths and concerns of the students in the class. The chart in Appendix K consists of five probing questions to guide this initial phase. By carefully addressing these five questions and reviewing specific classroom data, the teacher can identify classroom issues to consider that will identify a specific classroom problem. The following sections provide a guide to completing the questions, and an example of a completed form appears in Appendix K.

Strand: LANGUAGE — K–12 LA.D.1 Understands the nature of language LA.D.2 Understands the power of language			
	Criteria	Yes	No
1.	Uses language appropriate to situation/listener		
2.	Understands word meanings		
3.	Uses words effectively to get needs met		
4.	Uses a variety of vocabulary words when talking		
5.	Has trouble thinking (finding) the right word to say		
6.	Has trouble saying what he/she is thinking		
7.	Describes things to people		
8.	Sequences events in the correct order		
9	Uses correct grammar when talking		
10.	Uses complete sentences when talking		
11.	Expands on an answer or provides details		
12.	Explains what he/she has heard		

FIGURE 4.1
Curricular observation, informal assessment—Language

Probes for Problem Identification

Currently in my classroom, I am concerned about:

When responding to this statement, think about what you are noticing in your classroom that is drawing your attention. You may notice that student learning is not occurring as intended or planned. Your expectations for the student's learning should be related to the grade-level curriculum standards. Explicitly describe your concern related to student learning. You may have some work samples or initial assessments to refer to at this time.

Example of Noted Concerns

Mrs. Lue, a 3rd grade teacher, and Ms. Robinson, an ESE teacher, noticed that two of their students are having difficulties writing and reading independently. They entered the 3rd grade reading at the preprimer level. On writing rubrics scores, Donny and Julie scored Level 1, which is the lowest level of performance. Donny and Julie are performing significantly below their peers. Donny refuses to attempt any writing or reading assignment. He completely shuts down when asked to engage in any of these activities. Julie will attempt to read and write initially, but often gets frustrated and demands continuous support or behavior problems occur. Her writing is very immature, and she will rewrite the same message every day regardless of the writing prompt.

 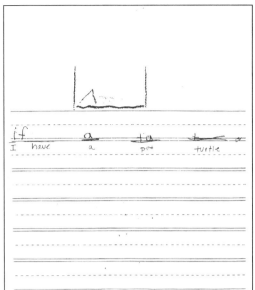

Writing Sample 1

Donny's writing prompt focused on telling a story about his family. He drew a picture detailing his family, but was unable to write a story.

Writing Sample 2

Donny wrote about his pet turtle. The teacher transcribed his story after Donny read his story aloud. (I have a pet turtle.)

FIGURE 4.2
Examples of Student Data: Donny's Initial Writing Samples

Example of Student Data: Observation of Julie's Writing

9/3/07, Language Arts

Activity: Writing in Journal

Julie wrote, "I love my pig. My pig is fun. I like to play. My pig likes to play. I love my pig."

After writing her message, she began to draw a picture of a pig playing in a park.

In order to investigate my concern, I need to collect information on:

After explicitly stating your concern, think about what information you want to gather based on the student learning needs. Why is learning breaking down? Why is there an issue that needs to be changed? To attempt to answer these questions, determine what kind of information you are missing or need to know.

Example of Needed Information

Donny and Julie are having significant difficulties learning to read and write. Mrs. Lue and Ms. Robinson asked themselves, "Why are they not reading and writing?" They decided to collect information on their reading readiness skills. The teachers already knew they were both reading instructionally at the pre-primer level, but did not have substantial information on why they were still reading at that level. Ms. Robinson and Mrs. Lue wanted to learn about Donny's and Julie's knowledge of letters and sounds, sight words, phonemic awareness and phonics abilities.

I will gather this information by collecting the following sources of data:

Once you have thought about what information you need, decide how you are going to collect it. What data sources or tools will you use to collect the information so that the problem to study can be accurately identified? Classrooms and schools are rich with data from assessments. Making time to carefully analyze different sources of information will help you determine your students' needs and strengths. Figure 4.3 provides a quick reference chart for data-collection sources, and the next sections provide information on other data sources that can be used to collect evidence on student learning.

Example of Using Data-Collection Sources

Ms. Robinson and Mrs. Lue reviewed their initial assessments in reading and writing. They chose to administer informal assessment surveys on phonemic segmentation, phonological awareness, and phonics (refer to several informal assessment templates in Appendices H, I, and J).

After analyzing my data, I found that my students are having difficulties with:

Specify the particular areas of weakness by stating student needs that were discovered after careful analysis of the data.

Example of Student Needs Statement

After administering and analyzing several data sources from the student records, observations, and classroom informal assessments, Ms. Robinson and Mrs. Lue found that Donny and Julie both had poor letter sound correspondence, weak phonemic awareness (segmenting and blending), a limited repertoire of sight words, and a lack of reading and writing strategies.

Student work samples	Rubrics	Informal assessments (Teacher-made or published)
Formal & informal observations	Grades, report cards, cumulative records	Interviews/surveys (student or parent)
Checklists	Formal tests	Performance assessments

FIGURE 4.3
Data collection sources

To meet my students' needs, I will focus my instruction on:

Once student needs have been stated, think about where you should focus your instruction to accelerate your students' learning. What evidence-based instructional strategies, resources, and materials could be used to meet the needs of the students? Will you require someone to assist you in locating or using other resources to meet these instructional needs? How much time and support will accelerate your students' learning?

Example of Decisions on Instructional Focus

Donny and Julie will require instruction specifically designed to target building letter/sound correspondence, phonemic awareness, and phonics in a comprehensive approach connecting reading to writing. Additional time and support using the evidence-based, instructional reading program used in the classroom may be needed. In addition, interventions specific to the identified instructional concerns may be also needed.

Review the content and use it as a guide as you complete the blank chart in Appendix K with respect to your concerns in this first phase of classroom instructional problem solving. A completed example in Appendix K reflects the analysis of the issues and concerns of the two teachers in this case study.

After reflecting on current concerns through these activities, identify some different instructional concerns to target for several students or the entire class. Choose one concern. It should be one that is most important for the students, is a priority learning need, will produce positive results for the students, and is aligned with the curricular standards and benchmarks for students to master at the grade level.

The Problem Statement

The last component of this phase is the problem statement. The problem statement will become the framework of the instructional problem solving and the resulting action plan for instruction and intervention. It will provide not only a description of the problem but also the goal for improvement related to the problem.

The problem statement must answer these four questions:

- Who is affected by the problem?
- What might be causing the problem?
- What is the goal for improvement?
- What might be done about the problem?

Once a classroom problem is identified, develop a problem statement. Begin to write down a clear, concrete specific description of the problem by answering the four questions above.

Summary of Phase 1

The problem-identification phase can be completed individually, collaboratively, or in conjunction with the members of the school's RtI team. As with each phase of classroom instructional problem solving, teachers will begin with their current instructional concerns. In the example in this chapter, coteachers in the 3rd grade are completing the problem-identification process.

During this phase, it is important to consider the student's characteristics and learning in relation to the current curricular standards and expectations. However, it is also important to reflect on the current instructional approaches and techniques used in the classroom. Teachers employ multiple instructional resources and teaching practices, and, as mentioned in earlier chapters, both the curricular content and the instructional practices affect student achievement. Therefore, the teacher must consider both content and instructional methods and identify evidence-based instructional approaches (e.g., direct instruction, peer tutoring, computer-assisted instruction).

Instructional strategies, size of the group, amount of time allocated for instruction, and resources are also important variables to consider during the problem-identification phase. These variables become especially important when developing the action plan, as they are some of the easiest to change to produce a positive impact on student achievement. A classroom instructional variables self-assessment is located in Appendix L, which can be used to notate specific information related to instruction in the classroom. Appendix M and N provide forms to use when identifying a classroom problem.

Reflection Questions:

- *Describe practices teachers should consider when identifying a classroom problem*
- *What are the four questions to address when creating a problem statement?*

Phase 2: Developing an Instructional or Intervention Plan

After investigating concerns and identifying a problem, the teacher turns attention to developing an instructional or intervention plan—a blueprint for immediate, intensive intervention within the classroom. This section names and describes the components to consider when completing the plans to meet the identified needs of the students, as aligned with curricular expectations. Checklists, timelines, and examples are provided to assist in completing the plan's development.

"Plan your work, then work your plan."

~ Anonymous

Reflection Questions:

- *What are the components of a classroom instructional problem-solving plan?*
- *Why are evidenced-based instruction and continuous progress monitoring important?*

- *How is a classroom instructional problem-solving plan and implementation schedule developed and used by teachers and others in the schools?*
- *What are three guiding principles for implementing a classroom instructional problem-solving plan?*

Major Components of RtI Related to Instruction

Response to Intervention is accomplished by developing, implementing, and monitoring instructional or intervention plans through problem solving. Before writing the specifics of the instructional or intervention plans, however, it is helpful to outline actions by answering the "what?" the "how?" and the "when?" The instructional or intervention action plan is a blueprint or framework for change within the classroom. Before creating the plan, take time to consider different instructional approaches to meeting students' instructional goals. Often, collaboration with other educators with diverse expertise and knowledge enhance the specific action plan created.

Three important and interrelated components affect the creation and implementation of the classroom action plan: evidence-based instruction, classroom implementation with high fidelity, and continuous progress monitoring. These components have an effect on curriculum, instruction, and assessment practices of teachers and are especially important in view of the increased focus on student achievement.

Evidence-based Instruction (Research-based or Scientifically-based Instruction)

Education contains a vast array of instructional resources, materials, and interventions that claim to improve student learning outcomes. More than ever, educators are expected to make instructional decisions including quality instruction. From policy makers to classroom teachers, educators need ways to separate misinformation from genuine knowledge and to distinguish scientific research from poorly supported claims. The authorization of the No Child Left Behind (NCLB) legislation (2002) brought a renewed emphasis on research validation processes to ensure that educators use the most effective instructional resources and interventions, based on scientific evidence. To meet the NCLB definition of scientifically based instruction, research must

- employ systematic, empirical methods that draw on observations or experiment;
- involve rigorous data analyses to test the stated hypotheses and justify general conclusions;
- rely on measurements or observational methods that provide valid data across evaluators and observers, and across multiple measurements and observations; and
- produce a report accepted by a peer-reviewed journal or approved by a panel of independent experts through a comparatively rigorous, objective, and scientific review.

The What Works Clearinghouse (http://www.w-w-c.org) was established by the federal government to review and identify the research and validation processes. Numerous educational organizations review research-validated instructional practices, programs, and interventions; a listing of educational websites appears in the Resources section of the Appendix. Teachers can use a simple set of questions to evaluate whether research validates the effectiveness of an instructional practice (NIFL, 2007):

- Has the study been published in a peer-reviewed journal or approved by a panel of independent reviewers?
- Have the results of the study been replicated by scientists?
- Is there consensus in the research community that the study's findings are supported by a critical mass of additional studies?

High-Fidelity Implementation

Fidelity of implementation refers to delivery of instruction in a way in which it was designed to be delivered (Gresham, MacMillan, Boebe-Frankenberger, & Bocian, 2000). At both the school and classroom level, instructional resources, methods and practices must be implemented by teachers the way the resources were designed and researched to improve student learning.

Although both common sense and research support the concept of fidelity of implementation to ensure success of an intervention to improve student achievement, the practical challenges associated with achieving high levels of fidelity are clear. These factors are related to complexity, resources required, teacher perceptions, and teacher skills (Reschly & Graham, 2006). Specific proactive practices can help ensure that fidelity of implementation occurs:

- Link interventions to improved student outcomes
- Specifically describe techniques, methods and components
- Clearly define responsibilities of specific persons
- Create a data system for measuring operations, techniques, and components
- Create a system for feedback and decision-making (formative)
- Create accountability measures for non-compliance (NRCLD, 2006).

Continuous Progress Monitoring

Ongoing progress monitoring is used to determine whether students are responding to the scientifically-based instructional program as part of the RtI framework. Within classroom instructional problem solving, data collected from multiple sources must be identified during action planning to ensure that student results will be monitored in any of the RtI tiers.

As described in earlier chapters, in the first instructional tier, the classroom teacher screens students to determine the likelihood of being at risk for poor achievement. Once these at-risk students are selected, the teacher monitors their progress periodically to determine whether they are responding appropriately to the instructional program within the classroom. If data show little to no change over a relatively brief period (e.g., 6 to 8 weeks), the teacher may recommend students for additional intervention and may proceed to a more intensive tier. Student performance over time illustrates whether the student is achieving appropriately, that is, responding well to the instructional program being delivered.

Two primary methods for monitoring progress are using robust indicators and curriculum sampling. Generating robust indicators involves administering measures on academic skills that are closely associated with performance of student measures. For example, a robust indicator in reading could be a series of 1-minute samples of oral reading fluency. In a curriculum sampling approach, student progress could be determined by monitoring performance on samples of items that represent the most critical curricular skills to be mastered by the end of the year (Deno, 2003; Stiggins, 1997).

Both robust indicators and curriculum sampling can be used successfully to gauge student progress over time in a particular subject area. Additional information about progress monitoring can be found at two national centers: Research Institute on Progress Monitoring (http://www.progressmonitoring.org) and National Center on Student Progress Monitoring (http://www.studentprogress.org).

Each of these three components—evidence-based instruction, classroom implementation with high fidelity, and continuous progress monitoring—is critical to the development, implementation, and monitoring of an instructional plan for improved student achievement through the classroom instructional problem-solving process. As teachers collect evidence—information and data—within their classrooms, their choices of resources and instructional materials and the fidelity of their use will affect student outcomes, which are subject to continuous monitoring of their learning progress. In addition, these components are equally important in each of the three tiers of the RtI process.

Developing a Classroom Instructional Plan

In developing an instructional or intervention plan, teachers and members of the RtI team reflect on, study, and answer a series of questions that focus their action planning to address the identified student needs. Given that classroom instructional problem solving may occur in any of the three tiers of the RtI process, the resulting plan will be referred to as both an instructional or intervention plan. This plan addresses the topics contained in Table 4.1.

Posing a Research Question

A research question is a carefully formed question that will be addressed by the implementation of the instruction or intervention plan. The research question must be even more specific than the problem statement and should focus on a measurable change or improvement. An effective research question must have four specific characteristics. In particular, it must

- identify a desired change in student learning,
- be specific and measurable,
- be answerable in a reasonable amount of time, and
- require an answer beyond a "yes" or "no" response.

Identifying the desired change

When composing a research question, specify the area of learning to improve or change. Avoid focusing on improving test scores as the desired change. (For example, "How can teaching research-based metacognitive strategies in content classes improve scores on state-administered assessments?" does not specify the area of learning to be addressed.) State-administered assessments could be used as one source for measuring student learning, but a change in assessment scores themselves should not be considered a target for research and intervention.

TABLE 4.1
Framework for an instructional or intervention plan.

Research question	What student learning will be studied? What scientifically-based instructional practices will be studied?
Learner outcomes	What specific student learning will occur related to the grade level curriculum standards and goals?
Instructional focus	What scientifically-based instructional practices will I implement that will focus on the classroom problem or issue to be changed? How will I assure fidelity of classroom implementation?
Data collection	What evidence do I need to collect? How will I collect the data? How often will I collect data? Are the data sources aligned to the instructional focus and learner outcomes? How will I assure this continuous progress monitoring?
Support	What support do I need from my colleagues? Who will assist me with fidelity of implementation?
Implementation schedule	How will I implement this plan? What is my timeline? When will I report back with the RtI team on student results?

A more appropriate example of a question directed at student learning might read, "How will modeling and providing practice in scientifically based metacognitive strategies effect my students' ability to monitor their comprehension when reading textbooks in content classes?"

Creating a specific and measureable question

The research question should be specific to student learning and the instructional practice that will be implemented. A research question guides the process, so specificity is important. In addition, specificity also supports improved fidelity of implementation. The more specific and measurable the research question, the more it leads to accurate data collection for progress monitoring. From the example cited, specific metacognitive strategies should be described as part of the research statement. Identifying the specific metacognitive strategies (e.g., paraphrasing the content using a specific scientifically-based program) will provide specific information about the research question as well as the specific content and progress monitoring. This information specific to curriculum, instruction, and progress monitoring will also be important if additional problem solving is needed to ensure student success in subsequent tiers.

Determining what is a reasonable amount of time

For practical reasons, a research question must be answerable in a reasonable amount of time. Remember to choose a topic of study that is important and attainable, and consider both curricular standards for units of study and progress monitoring assessments when deciding on "reasonableness" of time. Consider reasonable amounts of time in conjunction with units of study. For example, "How will modeling and providing practice in scientifically based metacognitive strategies in paraphrasing effect my students' ability to monitor their comprehension when reading textbooks in content classes during the next unit of study?"

Requiring more than a "yes" or "no" response

When wording a research question, begin a question with words such as "how," "when," or "why" Another example might be, "How can modeling through read-alouds improve students' abilities to organize, analyze, synthesize, and interpret what they read?"

Defining Learner Outcomes

When writing the instruction or intervention plan, think about the goals for student learning. After implementing the plan with fidelity, what improvement in achievement is expected for each of the students? Establishing high expectations and ambitious goals are important; however, the goals or outcomes must be attainable within a reasonable amount of time. In addition, while developing the research question and defining learner outcomes, continue to identify classroom informal assessments and progress monitoring assessments to use that will provide continuous feedback of student learning during implementation.

Studying and Developing an Instructional Focus

The instructional practice the teacher chooses to implement and monitor with a group of students is called the instructional focus. Finding an instructional focus may require some time, depending on the teacher's current knowledge, available resources, and teaching experiences with respect to the identified classroom problem. To address the student needs, teachers may need to learn and implement new methods, procedures, or programs. During this phase of classroom instructional problem solving, educators often study professional literature, attend professional development, engage in study groups and coaching, and consult knowledgeable support professionals within the school or district to continuously increase their knowledge of research-based instructional practices. Discussions during the RtI meetings with educators with diverse expertise will broaden the number of solutions described as plausible instructional techniques or intervention approaches, and collaboration among educators will provide knowledgeable resources and support during classroom implementation related to the instructional focus of the plan. At times, the instructional focus may be determined at the school or district level, as, for example, instructional decisions about the purchase and use of a particular research-based program.

The practices that are implemented through an instructional focus should directly target the identified classroom problem, and discussions should consider the specific proactive practices that help to ensure fidelity of implementation.

Identifying Data-Collection Sources

A critical part of this classroom instructional problem-solving process is data collection through continuous progress monitoring. Teachers continuously collect data to measure whether the instructional practices have had the desired effect, and they use information from the data to answer the instructional questions related to improved student learning. In addition, the data collected provide feedback on the instruction or intervention plan for the students at each tier of the RtI process. Decision making within the entire RtI process is based on progress monitoring of student results in each of the three tiers. Additional information on data collection and the various sources of data is in later sections of this book.

Determining the Level of Support

Educators rarely engage in classroom instructional problem solving without some support from their colleagues, support personnel, educational agencies, or university faculty. During planning, it is important to consider what information, resources, and support are needed to ensure fidelity of implementation and continuous progress monitoring. Whether the teacher is reflecting individually, collaborating with a colleague, or meeting with members of the RtI team, it is important to ask the following questions:

- Do I need further professional development?
- Will I need assistance with data collection and analyses?
- Could working with an instructional coach provide the support needed to implement scientifically based instructional programs with high fidelity?
- Will having opportunities to discuss the resources, plans, or assessment probes with colleagues provide a needed support system?

Creating an Instructional or Intervention Plan

The descriptions of the important instructional and assessment questions to consider within the classroom instructional problem-solving process lead to writing the instructional or intervention plan. In the case study described earlier, concerning the two students in the 3rd grade, the teachers developed a classroom instructional problem-solving plan developed based on the data collected from multiple sources. Their plan and a blank form for developing a plan appear in Appendix N.

Outlining Your Implementation Schedule

The final planning step for this phase is developing an implementation schedule. The implementation schedule lists the tasks to be completed, the beginning and ending dates for each task, and the necessary resources. It serves as a timeline of activities during implementation of the instructional plan. Critical to the implementation schedule is a follow-up meeting with the RtI team to present the progress-monitoring data after several weeks of implementation. At that follow-up meeting, discussions occur regarding the instructional and intervention plans to determine the effectiveness of the plan in terms of student outcomes as assessed through the continuous progress monitoring. Appendix O contains a blank implementation schedule as well as an example of an implementation schedule based upon the case study of two 3rd-graders.

Summary of Phase 2

The instructional or intervention plan is a blueprint for immediate, intensive instruction or intervention within the classroom. It is based on a carefully designed research question that is both specific and measureable, and is researchable in a reasonable amount of time. Checklists, timelines, and examples can assist in completing the plan's development.

Phase 3: Implementing an Instructional/Intervention Plan

Teaching makes numerous demands, and this section focuses on strategies and planning considerations to ensure high-fidelity implementation of the action plan or instructional strategies. Resources of scientifically based instructional methods will be shared. In addition, variables related to intensity of interventions will be described, especially in the reading content area. Specific examples, as well as several checklists, will be shared for consideration. In addition, discussions of support structures to ensure continued, high-quality implementation will be briefly described (e.g., observational forms, teacher study groups, team planning meetings, coaching, etc.).

"Both common sense and research support the concept of fidelity of implementation to ensure an intervention's successful outcome."

Reschly & Graham

Reflection Questions:

- *How are plans developed to address classroom concerns that are identified?*
- *How is fidelity of implementation assured within classrooms?*
- *What are sources of support to assure continued, high-quality implementation to ensure student successes?*

Classroom implementation of scientifically based instructional practices and interventions with fidelity is not only the most important element of the RtI process; it is also one the most difficult phases of this classroom instructional problem-solving process to achieve. Through the planning process, concerns about student achievement were discussed related to the screening assessment data available from a variety of sources. Collaboration among educators with diverse expertise elaborated both the current knowledge of student performance from classroom and assessment performance data and possible solutions. By consulting with the available educational references, members of the RtI problem-solving team reviewed the educational resources to ensure that they were scientifically based. Continuous progress measures were identified that would reliably collect student assessment data directly related to the identified classroom instructional problem. With the completion of the classroom instructional problem-solving plan, an implementation schedule was written to assure continuous progress monitoring and follow-up by the team.

Classroom instructional problem solving within the framework of RtI may represent a significant instructional shift for many educators. It requires coordination of processes at both the school and classroom level. Fidelity of implementation is critical if the classroom instructional plan is to be successful. Therefore, educators within districts, schools, and classrooms must advocate for the needed resources (e.g., programs, professional development, time for planning, etc.) to ensure that the scientifically based instructional programs and practices are implemented with high fidelity to achieve improved outcomes for students. "Essentially, if scientifically-based curriculum and instructional practices are implemented as they were designed, student outcomes should be better and more consistent than in previous years" (USDOE, 2006, pg. 45).

Implementing Your Plan

Therefore, when using the instructional or intervention plan in the classroom, it is important to implement the instructional practices with fidelity.

1. Implement the instructional practices consistently. To maintain the integrity of instruction, it is critical that implementation of the instructional practices and data collection occurs as described. Follow the plan as written.
2. Implement the instructional practices as designed. Scientifically based instructional methods, strategies, programs, and routines have been developed using information gathered from much research on their effectiveness. Deviations from guidelines for use of such instructional resources may affect the results within your classroom. Another way to ensure high-fidelity implementation in the classroom is to obtain feedback and guidance from a coach or another teacher who is knowledgeable in a specific instructional practice. See Appendix P for an "Essential Task List for Fidelity of Implementation," published through the Office of Special Education Programs (2006) as a guide to assure high fidelity implementation.
3. Monitor student results through continuous progress monitoring. Throughout this process, educators monitor student learning to determine the effect of the plan. The collection and analysis of data related to student achievement determine whether the instruction or intervention has been effective. In other words, data collected and analyzed during this process provide the answers to the instructional concerns in classrooms.

As described earlier, ensuring the fidelity of implementation is critical at both the school level (e.g., implementation of the RtI process) and the classroom level (e.g., implementation of both instruction and progress monitoring). Through a federal project sponsored through the Office of Special Education Programs (2006), researchers at the University of Kansas and Vanderbilt University have provided guidance related to assuring fidelity of implementation through each of the three tiers of the RtI process. To ensure fidelity within classrooms and schools, three dimensions to ensure fidelity have been conceptualized as follows:

1. *Method.* Various types of instructional programs and resources include various levels of support and information within them to support classroom implementation. For example, scripted lessons and resources that include all necessary materials for instruction provide the necessary supports for classroom implementation.
2. *Frequency.* The opportunities for implementation, instructional coaching, and professional feedback will vary the fidelity of classroom implementation. Factors such as experience, student characteristics and schedules for implementation affect this dimension.
3. *Support Systems.* Available and ongoing professional development and feedback during implementation affect the fidelity of classroom implementation (OSEP, 2006).

At the school level, resources to support teachers during implementation should be identified. For example, instructional and reading coaches with knowledge of the specific instructional programs or strategies may be available to model and provide feedback to the classroom teacher during initial implementation of the program. At the school level, administrators and members of the RtI and school improvement teams identify resources to ensure high-fidelity implementation. In addition, classroom teachers need time to plan (individually and with members of teams, such as grade level and RtI teams), time to analyze student progress monitoring data from instruction, and time to revise and redevelop resources to address identified concerns. School leaders can coach and/or facilitate instructional coaching of teachers in this process. Critical questions to address during this process include the following:

- How much time do students spend practicing what is being taught?
- How much direct instruction is used in a class period?
- Is reteaching determined by using reviewed student work?
- Which strategies are based on current research?
- How is the lesson aligned to school academic goals?
- How do lessons support state standards?
- What measures are used to determine student success?
- Is progress monitored continuously?
- Is instruction clear and focused?
- Do high expectations pertain to all students?

Teachers can benefit from seeing other teaching environments and observing colleagues teach. School leaders can facilitate these observations by

- allowing teachers to exchange classes and teach from someone else's plans,
- providing release time to observe in other classrooms or schools,
- funding conferences and workshops to support specific school goals,
- providing planning time for teachers to share what they observe and learn, and
- recognizing teacher successes.

Instructional resources such as programs and curriculum-based assessments should be identified and made available to classroom teachers. Continuous professional development, based on topics identified by classroom teachers during the RtI meetings, could be scheduled into the calendar of professional development offerings. For example, professional development sessions on topics related to understanding available data, such as results of state assessments and Dynamic Indicators of Basic Early Literacy Skills (DIBELS), use of school-adopted reading programs, and problem solving could be professional development sessions regularly in both large-group professional development meetings and study groups on grade-level teams.

Summary of Phase 3

Classroom implementation with scientifically based instructional methods based on the identified needs of students during the RtI process can often improve the results for all students. Teachers and other educators within the school ensure the successful mastery of the instructional goals by assuring classroom implementation with fidelity. Data collection through continuous student progress monitoring provides important feedback of student learning as a result of instruction. The next section provides an in-depth discussion of data collection and analysis during the classroom instructional problem-solving process.

Phase 4: Collecting and Analyzing Data

Numerous classroom-based assessments are available, and appropriate selection and application are important, so that assessments provide the information related to the specific classroom questions. In this chapter, questions and checklists are provided to assist in identifying the data-collection strategies (classroom assessments) related to the instructional need identified in the previous phases of the RtI tiers. Several data-collection sources for monitoring student learning related to the instructional or intervention plan are also described. Numerous examples and resources will be shared.

"Data provide the power to…make good decisions, work intelligently, work effectively and efficiently, change things in better ways, know the impact of our hard work, help us prepare for the future, and know how to make our work benefit all children."

~Victoria L. Bernhardt

Reflection Questions:

- *Do the assessment instruments and methods selected, measure the described outcome?*
- *Are the assessment instruments and methods selected easy to administer and score consistently?*
- *How is continuous progress monitoring completed in a consistent and reliable way?*
- *Have multiple sources of classroom data and assessments been identified?*

Curriculum, Instruction, and Assessment

Curriculum, instruction, and assessment are integral and interrelated components of the teaching and classroom instructional problem-solving processes within the RtI framework. Teachers must be able to articulate classroom expectations contained in the curriculum standards, since curriculum knowledge creates the framework of the content to be learned by the students in the class (Bernhardt, 1998). The instructional focus, then, is the instructional practices and materials used by the teacher to teach curricular expectations.

Assessment provides the data needed to determine whether students are learning and meeting the curricular goals. Teachers collect evidence through assessments in the continuous progress monitoring process, and they use it to make instructional decisions.

Reflective Questions:

- *Based on my evidence, do I continue implementing the instruction?*
- *Do I modify my instruction to better meet the needs of my students?*
- *Does the evidence suggest that the practice is not making an impact?*
- *If so, will I implement another approach?*

The information received through data collection guides the classroom instructional problem-solving process and instruction and interventions needed for students in the classroom.

How to Gather Evidence on Student Learning

> *"Using a variety of assessment tools and approaches gives us more confidence that decisions are based on accurate evidence. Gathering evidence of student learning is a primary function of teaching."*
>
> *~Aitken et al.*

Gathering assessment data from many sources can help build a complete picture of student learning and abilities and measure progress related to the impact of classroom instruction. Using only one form of assessment can provide a misleading snapshot of individual ability on only one day; whereas gathering evidence from many different sources over a longer period of time yields a broader and deeper understanding of student knowledge and learning. In research terminology, the process of collecting multiple sources of data for every problem (phenomenon) or issue being studied is called triangulation (Sagor, 2005). Triangulating data may seem time-consuming and overwhelming at first, but it is actually time-efficient and more effective than a single collection because students' needs are more explicitly and clearly defined during the instructional process (pre-assessment, continuous progress monitoring, and outcome).

The following guidelines have been published by the National Council of Teachers of Mathematics (NCTM, 2001). NCTM stated that to be useful, assessments should

- match what students have been studying;
- focus on important content rather than trivia;
- yield useful information, not just "scores";
- use clear and helpful criteria; and
- provide a complete picture of students' learning and abilities.

> *"Schools are naturally data-rich environments, and simply opening our eyes to some of the most frequently used and easily obtainable sources of data can make planning the data collection process much easier."*
>
> *~Sagor*

Instructional problem solving should become a part of the classroom teacher's daily work, so that selecting the data-collection strategies simply emerges from thinking about life in the classroom/school and the ways life in the classroom or school can be naturally captured as data (Dana & Yendol-Silva, 2003). Put another way, within the instructional process, educators are continuously gathering and using data from their classrooms throughout the day (Allen et al., 2001).

Reflection Questions:

In selecting data-collection strategies, think about assessments already in place in your classroom and school and reflect on the following questions:

- *What information do I need to collect to measure student learning aligned to my instructional focus?*
- *What data-collection sources will provide me with the needed information?*
- *Are the data-collection sources easy to administer, gather, and analyze?*

Classroom Data-Collection Tools

Continuous progress monitoring using various assessments can be a complex and intensive process, and the selection of an appropriate tool is essential. The types of assessment tools can be divided into two main categories, direct and indirect (Gresham, 1989).

Direct assessment tools

Direct assessments are clearly defined in operational terms: Teachers and other educators observe the teaching, intervention, or student behavior to determine the percentage of occurrence, accuracy, or incidence. Examples of direct assessment measures include checklists used in observations, curriculum-based informal tests, and progress-monitoring standardized measures (i.e., DIBELS).

Observations   In observational assessment, educators watch students and record the behaviors or actions seen in a qualitative (written) or quantitative (numerical) form. Taking notes on observations is a very common data-collection approach. To document observations, it is helpful to record observations in an organized manner. Different formats may include checklists, anecdotal records, and grids or charts. Appendixes Q, R, S, and T offer examples of observation recording forms, and NCTM (2003) suggests the following to ensure that observations are manageable and useful:

- Determine what you want to assess.
- Decide which students you will observe.
- Decide how you will record your information.
- Plan activities for students to perform while you observe (Aitken et al., 2003)

Checklists   Checklists are an efficient way to record observations of student learning related to a specific objective or objectives. When creating a checklist, describe the event as explicitly and clearly as possible. For example, when observing student performance, mark the checklist with notations that reflect whether the student was able to perform the specific objective(s). Additional notes may be written, if applicable. Checklists can be used to record data on an individual student, small group, or whole class.

Checklists can be created that are directly related to the curriculum to be mastered by the teacher. Checklists also collect student behaviors, such as engagement, social skills, and disruptions. There are also numerous checklists available that correlate to the scientifically based instructional programs as informal assessments for teachers to use during instruction. (See the writing continuum checklist in Appendix T as an example).

Tests Criterion-referenced tests and norm-referenced tests are two common sources of data that are used in classrooms and schools on a continuous basis. The criterion-referenced test is used frequently to measure student learning related to a particular objective or criterion. Test items usually sample sequential skills, enabling a teacher not only to know the specific point at which to begin instruction but also to plan those instructional aspects that follow directly in the curricular sequence (Salvia & Ysseldyke, 1998). Some examples of criterion-referenced tests include teacher-made tests, published tests (curriculum or resources), and curriculum-based assessments (see Appendix U for a sample). Refer to the Resource section in the Appendix for numerous resources related to reading resources available for educators.

Norm-referenced tests (standardized tests) compare the performance of individual students to their peers (a norm group). The score allows schools and teachers to rank individual students. This form of assessment is not administered on a regular basis such as the criterion-referenced test.

Indirect Assessments

Indirect assessment measures include methods of data collection that report less-quantifiable information. Included in this type of assessment are anecdotal records, rating scales and self-reports, interviews, and reviews of permanent products and records (e.g., grades). Of the indirect methods, permanent product assessment, such as portfolios and work products, is thought to be the most reliable and accurate. Several examples of indirect assessment measures follow.

Anecdotal Records Anecdotal records are written narratives of teacher observations of their students. Teachers record their important observations either to note student progress or to inform instruction. When anecdotal notes are recorded methodically across time, they become very useful tools for reflecting on children's progress within a given time span (Sagor, 2005). Anecdotal records can be documented several ways, including on note cards, notebook paper, the computer, charts, and so on.

Note Card Example

November 15, 2007

During a read-aloud with the focus on rhyming, Susan and Donny were demonstrating difficulty with producing rhymes. Both were able to identify rhyming pairs at an independent level without any support.

Charts and grids provide an efficient way to organize the observation and reporting during the writing of the anecdotal records and can be used to note performance of individual students, small groups, or the whole class. Brief notations are recorded on student performance related to a task.

Chart Example

Name: Susan

Date	Anecdote	Action
11/15/03	Susan was able to identify rhyming pairs, but demonstrated difficulty with producing rhymes.	Model and scaffold in the areas of rhyme production

Grid Example

Date: 11/15/03

Objective: Rhyme production

Name: Susan	Name: Donny	Name: Carlos	Name: Isabel
Name: Jason	Name: Jordan	Name: Marquis	Name: Kelly
Name: Anthony	Name: Ricardo	Name: Linh	Name: Jeremiah

Interviews and Conversations Interviews with students can provide helpful information regarding students' perceptions of their own learning and knowledge. Informal interviews are a question and answer session conducted by the teacher with an individual student. Harp (2000) stated that interviews conducted during conferences can give teachers a great deal of insight into students' thinking. In addition, questioning and engaging in conversation with students while working on a specific task can provide teachers with rich data on the student's immediate understanding.

Questions in interviews or conversations should be asked in an open-ended format to elicit responses other than "yes" or "no." An example would be, "What do you do when you have difficulty understanding what you read?" Hubbard and Power (1993) stated that asking students why and how they do their work and getting them to analyze those processes themselves helps teachers enlist their students as coresearchers. When recording your students' responses, you may want to write their answers on an interview question sheet or on a chart or grid for documentation. Please refer to Appendix V for another sample of student interviews related to their learning.

Student Work Examples of student work can be a powerful source of data for teachers. Hubbard and Power (1999) state that student work is tangible evidence of what kids are able to do and provide a range of responses kids make to different learning tasks. Student work may include writing samples, student journals, homework assignments, reports, math performance tasks, and artwork.

Two vehicles for evaluating student work are portfolios and rubrics. A portfolio approach involves collecting and analyzing samples of individual student work over a period of time. The samples of work, which consist of completed work samples used for assessment or evaluation purposes, are organized in a binder or notebook and may include (Harp, 2000):

- Reading
  - Copies of reading assessments
  - Reading logs
  - Reading journal
  - Anecdotal records
  - Audiotape of student's reading

- Writing
  - Essays, reports, stories, letters, projects, poetry
  - Finished pieces that illustrate ability to write in various genres
  - Several drafts of a piece and a final version
  - Pieces that illustrate a particular skill, such as staying on topic or providing supportive details.

A rubric is a set of scoring guidelines for evaluating students' work (Wiggins, 1998), consisting of scales that define levels of performance for specific tasks. Educators use rubrics to assess students' performance as high, average, and low quality based on a set of standards. General rubrics describe the criteria of successful work in general terms and can be applied to a variety of tasks or problems. Specific rubrics reflect the same criteria as general rubrics do, but they include much more detail about specific tasks rather than sets of tasks (NCTM, 2003). Rubrics should be shared with students before they are assessed, so they are aware of the expectations.

Grades, Report Cards, Cumulative Records   Calhoun (2002) refers to grades, report cards, and cumulative records as "existing archival sources of data." These archives can provide a history of your students' learning and schooling as well as reflecting their progress as new documents become available. Within these school and teacher files, you may find information on student grades, discipline referrals, standardized test reports, past work samples, etc.

Data collection assessments and processes must be of high quality to ensure credible data collection related to student results. To ensure this quality, the following three questions should be addressed:

- Do the assessment instruments and methods selected measure what you want to measure (are they valid measures)?
- Are the assessment instruments and methods selected easy to administer and score consistently (are they reliable)?
- Are the data collected from several sources, convincing, and thorough (are they susceptible to triangulation)?

Summary of Phase 4

Assessment and data collection are important throughout instructional problem solving. Teachers and other educators collect and analyze assessment data daily during screening and prescribe additional assessments to further diagnose the presenting instructional concerns, monitor the instructional progress, or summarize the outcomes for a specific period of time (e.g., length of intervention, grading period, annual progress, etc.). By asking questions, collecting data, intervening, and continuously monitoring student progress, teachers, like doctors, prescribe instruction and interventions to meet the instructional and behavioral needs for all students.

Putting the Pieces Together

The case study contained in the Appendix is used in professional development of teachers and speech-language pathologists as a means to use the information and practice the skills of instructional problem solving within the state of Florida (FDOE, 2004b). The case study concerns a 3rd-grade student, with educational history and data from assessments from kindergarten. Summary documents are included, as well as additional forms to use for developing a classroom instructional plan for the student. The case study can be used by individuals, team members, or RtI team members as they identify resources and practice all of the components for efficient and effective instructional problem-solving within the framework of RtI. See Appendix W for a simple form to summarize instructional needs and planning.

Summary

While finding time to learn about the students and their backgrounds, skills, and abilities can be difficult, ultimately each teacher's concern is whether all students in the classroom are learning. Teachers must continuously observe, think about, and analyze student learning relative to mastery of grade-level curricular standards and expectations, and the classroom instructional problem-solving process provides the means for identifying specific instructional needs based on student data. Basing instructional decisions on classroom data leads to instruction that targets the identified needs of the students.

The last chapter of this book discusses the final phase of the classroom instructional problem-solving process, which is using and sharing results. This phase focuses on using data to make instructional decisions about the next steps of this process, in relation to the RtI framework within the school.

CHAPTER 5

WHY? REVISITED: Rationale—Improved Student Learning Through Classroom Instructional Problem Solving

Overview

Completing the continuous improvement cycle through the instructional problem-solving process requires examining the student results related to the instructional and research goals set at the outset. A decision-making matrix of instructional decisions provides the framework for deciding on how to celebrate the successful completion, continue the plan with revisions, or review phases of the plan. A self-assessment rubric of quality indicators for the action research process provides thoughtful considerations about the implementation process of the action research plan. Final discussions connect the outcomes of the action research plan with the identified rationale and uses for completing this research.

Sharing the results of the action research and the student results with parents, other educators, principals, and others is often appropriate. Aligning the results of the intervention plan with the tiers of the RtI process will guide this process.

> *"People without information cannot act.*
> *People with information cannot help but act."*
> ~Ken Blanchard

Determining Next Steps

After planning, teaching, and collecting data, school-based professionals must analyze the results of the instructional plan and make instructional decisions based on the findings as an integral process within RtI. The analyzed data will answer a critical question in the RtI process—that is, "Where do I go next?" The assessment data collected through continuous progress monitoring will assist the RtI team members in determining the next actions, whether these are to continue with current practices, revise the instructional plan to more specific interventions, or report the results of student successes.

The following questions help in determining the next steps:

- Are students benefiting from the instructional focus that I have planned and implemented?
- Was the classroom problem solved?
- Did the instructional focus align with my students' needs?
- Were all of the phases of the process followed?
- Was the plan completed as written (with the materials and time dedicated as outlined in the implementation schedule)?
- Were all the necessary materials (personnel and resources) available? Did I receive the support I need?
- Did the information (data) collected from the students provide the necessary evidence about the results of the efforts to solve the problem?

If the answer to these questions is "yes" and assessment data show improved student learning that met the stated goal(s) for improvement, it is time to share the results and identify the next classroom problem for study. Appendix X provides an example of a report of instruction that produced improved student outcomes in reading.

If the answer to the questions is not "yes," then the findings may offer two choices: continue to implement the plan or revise the plan to consider more intensive interventions.

When considering what steps of intervention are suggested by the student data collected after high-fidelity instruction based on the collaboratively developed plan, think about the instructional practices that are being used to solve the identified classroom problem.

Reflection Questions:

- *Are you finding that students are making progress with the current instructional focus?*
- *If so, have the students met instructional expectations?*
- *Has progress been made but the goal(s) for improvement left unmet?*

If a school decides that the first tier of instructional classroom problem solving represents the first level of intervention, then Tier 2 may include instruction in even smaller groups, employ more minutes of instruction, or use a more intensive program. If the members of the RtI team are satisfied with the current evidence and rate of student progress, continuing the current instructional focus without altering the instructional plan may be the professional decision to make.

School schedules and unexpected circumstances may cause an interruption or delays to the instructional plans. In this event, it is wise to take time to refocus and continue with the initial plan of action according to the implementation schedule. It may be advisable to increase the intensity or "dosage" of the instruction with respect to the amount of time dedicated to the goals of instruction or a smaller number of students in the small group. Both of these variables will provide additional academic engaged time and opportunities to respond for feedback from peers and the teacher.

Most often, Tier 2 interventions are implemented by the classroom teacher through flexible grouping and differentiated instruction or by other school personnel with sufficient expertise in the area of the student's needs. For example, a speech-language pathologist may suggest techniques in language development related to the reading skills to be developed. Revising instructional and personnel variables can often enhance and maximize the positive results.

Many factors contribute to the decision of how to proceed. Each subsequent tier represents a more intensive level of instruction, offering changes in instructional programs, increased frequency, intensity, or duration of instruction to provide more instructional and behavioral supports. Also, more frequent or different assessment probes may need to be administered. If student learning is questionable, has the classroom problem been identified correctly? Collaboration with knowledgeable colleagues during RtI team meetings will answer this question and re-identify the classroom problem.

Another action that may be necessary is revision of the instructional focus. Take time to reflect on the instructional practices and analyze the collected data to determine whether students are learning.

Reflection Questions:

- *Are the scientifically based resources and programs meeting the instructional goal and focus for the identified student(s)?*
- *Is there high fidelity with the implementation of the instructional focus?*
- *Will intensifying instruction result in improvements?*
- *Is there another instructional approach?*

Again, collaborating with a coach, mentor, teacher, or support personnel of the RtI team may prove helpful in determining the next instructional steps. The process of continuous classroom instructional problem-solving continues through Tiers 2 and 3, when RtI team members will make decisions regarding referral for additional programmatic services, including, perhaps, a comprehensive evaluation to determine the possibility of a disability.

At this point, all federal, state, and local procedures to safeguard the specific rights for students and their families will apply. As the special-education process is beyond the scope of this book, the following section concentrates on the teacher's decisions at the follow-up RtI meetings.

Sharing and Reporting Your Results

After assessment data have been analyzed in the context of established curricular goals and the instructional focus, it is time to share and report the results. Results can be reported in a variety of formats, depending on the audience and purpose of the reporting. Several options are available for this reporting.

Individual Reporting

Individual reporting is probably the most common way results are reported within schools. Teachers complete an accurate report of the individual student's level of achievement of curricular goals and place the report in the student's folder, file, portfolio, and other records. Other data collected through the classroom instructional problem-solving process are easily reported through school, district, and state accountability reporting systems, underscoring the importance of aligning the instructional plans to curricular goals.

Graphic Representations of Results

Presentation of data must be clear and meaningful, with confidentiality protected so that no one individual student can be identified. Carefully prepared charts, graphs, tables, and target lines will present the findings in a clear fashion. Computer-assisted software for analyzing, graphing, and charting data is readily available.

Discussions and Presentations With Teachers

A very effective strategy for disseminating results of classroom instruction is the use of discussions with other educators within grade levels, instructional teams, or the school. Discussions provide personal professional development directly related to educational issues identified at the school. When presenting this information, report only on the expectations for student learning and present some of the data collected. Again, tables, charts, and graphs may be effective tools to use with the audience. Specific questions to facilitate dialogue include the following:

- Do you think that what I believe occurred is what really happened?
- As you look at the data, do you think any unplanned results occurred?
- In what ways do you think the quality of education for my students improved during this time?
- What did you learn from these results?
- What will be the next steps for you? For your students?

Of course, the most important evaluations, reflections, and decisions are those of each teacher and educator involved with the process, since the results of the classroom research will be a basis for making informed decisions about teaching and learning for all students. Once the data are compiled, analyzed, shared, and discussed, it is critical that teachers and educators ask these core questions:

- How was the quality of instruction improved for my students?
- How was my understanding of my teaching changed and improved?
- Are my students meeting the academic and behavioral goals?

The answers to these questions will lead into the cycle of continuous improvement—creating new goals for improvement and plans for continued instruction and intervention based on evidence of student learning. As each teacher uses problem-solving to address classroom needs within the framework of RtI, each student will learn.

Written Reports and Professional Articles

Teacher research continues to increase knowledge within the teaching profession, and reporting research disseminates important findings and advances the practice of education (Sagor, 2005). Often, classroom teachers who have designed a research plan, implemented it, and collected student data to determine instructional effectiveness will describe findings through a report or professional article. Publishing results of instruction becomes a form of professional development for others. As mentioned, Appendix X contains an example of the results of instruction in a report format for a professional journal, and the instructional plan and its implementation can be outlined in the elements shown on the template in Appendix Y. Whichever format the teacher chooses for reporting results, it is important to show the results informally (e.g., school records, reports) or more formally (e.g., journal articles).

How Can Teachers Be School Leaders Within the RtI Process?

Lacking a comprehensive blueprint for school districts to follow at this time, teachers must be proactive in establishing, continuing, or improving RtI as both an early-intervention process and a data-collection process that can add important information during a comprehensive evaluation for special education. The success of RtI will depend, to a great extent, on whether it is executed by highly trained professionals who have a firm understanding of the process. The following suggestions are made here to encourage activity on the part of educators:

- Study the issues of RtI on your own. The resources listed in the Resource section of the Appendix are helpful for solidifying your individual understanding of the RTI theoretical framework.
- Attend regional or state trainings on RtI. Campaign for others to join you, including other teachers, reading specialists, school psychologists, and administrators.
- Contact local regional resource centers for up-to-date research information and model schools in your area. (See the Resource section in the Appendix for a list of the regional resource centers in the United States.)
- Examine current school methods and programs to determine whether any recommended or already used commercial programs are a good overall match. Review the criteria for instructional materials, products, and resources considered to be "scientifically based." Compare the current resources and instructional materials used against the published criteria.
- Consider the various procedures and roles of each team member of an RtI school team. Many school systems already have in place something close to an RtI system. For example, some schools have a child-study team or a prereferral team composed of general education teachers, reading specialists, school psychologists, and special education staff. Roles may shift in the RtI model and must be explicit for RtI success. However, it is important to first examine current school and classroom practices for alignment.
- Endorse professional development related to implementing the RtI process with fidelity within the school for personnel involved in the process.
- Share expertise in instructional methods and strategies used to teach struggling students. Collaboration with other members of the faculty and staff will be essential to successfully implementing problem-solving approaches.

- Promote the use of scientifically based assessments as data sources to monitor the RtI program and determine whether it is being implemented successfully.

Summary

As a systematic, data-based method for identifying, defining, and resolving students' academic difficulties, Response to Intervention (RtI) offers a model for preventing academic failure among students. RtI relies on the skills of professionals from different disciplines to develop and evaluate instruction and intervention plans that significantly improve the performance of students through an instructional problem-solving (action research) process. The methods and approaches presented in this book allow data-driven instruction and interventions to be integrated into the curriculum to meet the specific, data-driven needs of individual students. The result is improvement in all students' achievement, thereby meeting the goal of Response to Intervention. To review important concepts and understandings, see Appendix Z for critical questions related to classroom instructional problem solving. Additional information from resources and websites is included in Appendix Z as well.

CASE STUDY: Rosa

Introduction

Rosa is an eight-year-old female in the third grade. Her teacher reports that she is struggling with the curriculum. Rosa moved with her family from Mexico and was non-English speaking when she entered kindergarten; she did not attend pre-kindergarten. Rosa's home language is Spanish. Her parents speak very little English and are illiterate in both Spanish and English.

Rosa's teacher reports that she does well with math computation, but is having difficulty with all other subjects including reading. She appears to decode well, but struggles with curriculum measures such as unit tests in the reading curriculum. Rosa has been promoted every year since kindergarten. She received ESOL services from K–2nd grade, but passed the IDEA proficiency test (an English-language proficiency test administered to non-native speakers) at the end of 2nd grade so she no longer receives these services. Rosa has never been referred for exceptional education services.

Education History

Kindergarten

Rosa has been attending South Street Elementary School since kindergarten. South Street is a Title 1 funded school and also a Reading First school. Rosa was enrolled in kindergarten and also received pull-out ESOL services owing to her score on the IDEA proficiency test.

ESOL Services	
Test	*Results*
IDEA Proficiency Test	Non-English Speaking

DIBELS		
Assessment Period	*Measures*	*Score & Score Interpretations*
Assessment 1	Initial Sound Fluency (ISF)	0, High Risk
	Letter Naming Fluency (LNF)	0, High Risk
Assessment 2	Initial Sound Fluency (ISF)	14, Medium Risk
	Letter Naming Fluency (LNF)	7, High Risk
Assessment 3	Initial Sound Fluency (ISF)	33, Low Risk
	Letter Naming Fluency (LNF)	30, Low Risk
	Phoneme Segmentation Fluency (PSF)	35, Low Risk
	Nonsense Word Fluency (NWF)	18, Low Risk

DIBELS (continued)		
Assessment 4	Letter Naming Fluency (LNF)	34, Medium Risk
	Phoneme Segmentation Fluency (PSF)	49, Above Average
	Nonsense Word Fluency	22, Medium Risk

Classroom-Based Assessments	
Skill	*End of Year Results*
Letter Naming	Grade Appropriate
Sound Identification	Grade Appropriate

Year-End Outcomes Test	
Test	*Score & Score Interpretation*
PPVT	Percentile Rank 16, High Risk

1st Grade

Rosa continued attending South Street Elementary School, receiving pull-out services for ESOL. She made improvements in mastering English, but struggled with reading for understanding and answering questions in class.

ESOL Services	
Test	**Results**
IDEA Proficiency Test	Limited English Speaking

DIBELS		
Assessment Period	**Measures**	**Score & Score Interpretations**
Assessment 1	Letter Naming Fluency (LNF)	43, Low Risk
	Phoneme Segmentation Fluency (LNF)	40, Low Risk
	Nonsense Word Fluency (NWF)	31, Low Risk
	Oral Reading Fluency (ORF)	15, Above Average
Assessment 2	Phoneme Segmentation Fluency (LNF)	39, Low Risk
	Nonsense Word Fluency (NWF)	47, Above Average
	Oral Reading Fluency (ORF)	25, Above Average

DIBELS (continued)		
Assessment 3	Phoneme Segmentation Fluency (PSF)	52, Above Average
	Nonsense Word Fluency (NWF)	49, Medium Risk
	Oral Reading Fluency (ORF)	32, Low Risk
Assessment 4	Phoneme Segmentation Fluency (PSF)	62, Above Average
	Nonsense Word Fluency	61, Low Risk
	Oral Reading Fluency (ORF)	40, Low Risk

Classroom-Based Assessments	
Skill	**End of Year Results**
Phonics Inventory	Grade Appropriate
Sight Words	Grade Appropriate

Year-End Outcomes Test	
Test	**Results & Interpretation**
PPVT	Percentile Rank 18, High Risk
Stanford 10 Reading Comprehension	Percentile Rank 45, Low Risk

2nd Grade

Rosa was promoted to second grade. She continued to attend South Street Elementary and received pull-out ESOL services. Rosa received the core curriculum (grade-level initial reading instruction that is systematic and explicit), including guided reading (small group instruction using materials at the students' reading level) focusing on comprehension strategies. Rosa was reading below-level materials in her guided reading group. She received no other interventions for reading or math. She continued to have no difficulty with math computation, but had difficulty understanding written math problems.

ESOL Services	
Test	**Results**
IDEA Proficiency Test	FES: Fluent English Speaking

DIBELS		
Assessment Period	**Measures**	**Score & Score Interpretations**
Assessment 1	Nonsense Word Fluency (NWF)	65, Low Risk
	Oral Reading Fluency (ORF)	39, Medium Risk
DIBELS (continued)		
Assessment 2	Nonsense Word Fluency (NWF)	50, Low Risk
	Oral Reading Fluency (ORF)	67, Low Risk
Assessment 3	Nonsense Word Fluency (NWF)	53, Low Risk
	Oral Reading Fluency (ORF)	80, Low Risk
Assessment 4	Nonsense Word Fluency (NWF)	55, Low Risk
	Oral Reading Fluency (ORF)	92, Low Risk

Year-End Outcomes Test	
Test	**Score & Score Interpretation**
PPVT	Percentile Rank 4, High Risk
Stanford 10 Reading Comprehension	Percentile Rank 3, High Risk

Stanford 10 Achievement Tests	
Total Reading	13%, Stanine 3
Word Study (Multiple choice that consists of Structural Analysis: compound words, inflectional endings, and contractions; Phonetic Analysis-Consonants: single consonants, consonant clusters, and consonant digraphs; and Phonetic Analysis-Vowels: short vowels, long vowels, and other vowel sounds)	24%, Stanine 4
Reading Vocabulary (Multiple choice that consists of Reading Vocabulary: synonyms, multiple meaning words, and words in context)	28%, Stanine 4
Reading Comprehension (Multiple choice that includes reading text that is recreational, textual, and functional; understanding of specific detail, action, reason and sequence; interpretation of inference and extending meaning; critical analysis; and strategies)	7%, Stanine 2
Language (Multiple choice that includes Mechanics: capitalization, punctuation, and usage; Expression: sentence structure and content and organization)	13%, Stanine 3
Spelling (Multiple choice that includes sight words, phonetic principles, consonant and vowel sound; structural principles; inflection endings)	18%, Stanine 3

3rd Grade

Rosa entered the third grade with an IDEA proficiency score of FES (fluent English-speaking) and was dismissed from the ESOL pull-out program. At the end of the second grading period Rosa continues to struggle with reading (unsatisfactory on her unit tests, below level in guided reading) and written language assignments (limited word choice). Because of her performance, the reading coach administered the Diagnostic Assessment of Reading (DAR) to gather more information as to Rosa's deficits.

Diagnostic Assessment of Reading (DAR)	
Sub-tests	*These are grade levels.*
Word Recognition	Level (3)
Oral Reading	(Accuracy) Level (3)
Silent Reading Comprehension	Level (3)
Spelling	Level (2)
Word Meaning	Level (1)

DIBELS		
Assessment Period	*Measures*	*Score & Score Interpretations*
Assessment 1	Oral Reading Fluency (ORF)	91, Low Risk
Assessment 2	Oral Reading Fluency (ORF)	67, Medium Risk

For further assistance, the teacher consulted with the school's speech-language pathologist (SLP), who suggested that the teacher complete a language checklist. The teacher marked the following as being of serious concern (++).

Reading:

- Studies for tests effectively++
- Follows written directions without difficulty++

Writing:

- Uses adequate spelling++
- Uses appropriate grammatical complexity++
- Can perform on essay tests++

Speaking:

- Uses appropriate specific vocabulary++
- Uses and "gets" humor appropriately++
- Can express opinions clearly++
- Has no trouble finding words during speaking++

Listening:

- Can understand class lectures++
- Understands idioms, proverbs, slang in context++
- Can answer questions based on lecture and other orally presented material++

Identifying Language and Reading Needs & Instructional Planning

Student Name:_____ Grade:_____ Date of Plan:_____

Date of RtI Meeting:_____ Teacher:_____ Speech Language Pathologist:_____

Reading Coach:_____ School Psychologist:_____ Other:_____

School-Based Assessments and Classroom Screening Results		What reading diagnostic(s) were administered and analyzed?	Instructional Planning & Progress Monitoring Monitoring Instruction	
School-Based Assessment Results	What do we know?	Name of diagnostic(s):	Reading Component(s)	Target Skills:
Classroom Screening Results		Results:	Learning Outcome(s)	Strategy/ Intervention:
Core Instruction and Results	What do we need to know?	Student's strengths and needs:	Instruction Timeline	Progress Monitoring
		Strengths: Needs:		

(See Appendix W, as well.)

Identifying a Classroom Problem

Name(s):

School:

Grade Level:

Problem Statement: Compose a problem statement specifically describing *who is affected, supported causes of the problem,* the *goal for improvement,* and *what might be done about the problem* as stated. Provide as much specific information as possible.

Classroom Instructional Problem-Solving Plan		
Name(s):	School:	Grade Level:
Research Question: Pose a question that will focus your study. Be sure to include what student learning will occur and what instructional practices will be implemented.		
Learning Outcomes: What specific student learning will occur?		
Instructional Focus: Describe the specific instructional practice(s) that will be implemented and studied. Specify when and how the practice will be implemented.		
Data Collection: Specify the data sources that you will use that are aligned to the classroom problem.		

How often will you collect the data?

Data Source 1: (What & How?)

Data Source 2: (What & How?)

Data Source 3: (What & How?)

Support: What support will you need from your colleagues?

Implementation Schedule

Tasks	Timeline Beginning/Ending	Resources

Appendixes

Appendix A

Collaborative Roles in RtI Process

Although the membership of RtI school-based teams may vary, the following disciplines are most often represented:

Principal or Assistant Principal: administrative leadership and facilitation

General Education Teacher: knowledgeable of curriculum and instruction

Reading Teacher: expertise of reading process, resources, and the like

School Psychologist: test interpretation and behavioral data

Speech Therapist: expertise in language development and articulation

Special Education Teacher: knowledge of specialized programs and resources for students with disabilities and experiencing difficulties in school

Appendix B

Key Characteristics of Problem-solving

As you read through each item, reflect on your current understanding and skills needed for problem-solving within the schools. Consider how important each of these understanding and skills are the total functioning of the school-based RtI team. Discuss your answers and feelings with other members of the team, if appropriate.

_____ 1. Do I best serve the students that I teach?

_____ 2. Are there students whose needs are not being met?

_____ 3. Am I willing to discuss various instructional approaches and interventions with others?

_____ 4. Am I curious to learn more about teaching and student learning?

_____ 5. Am I open to learn how I can improve my practice for all students?

_____ 6. Is there open communication and trust within our team?

_____ 7. Is there open communication and trust within our school?

_____ 8. Do we believe in a model of continuous improvement?

_____ 9. Is there collaboration among members of the team?

_____10. Do I build rapport by communicating with a caring attitude?

_____11. Do I monitor both my verbal and non-verbal behaviors?

_____12. Do I encourage feedback by asking reflective questions?

_____13. Do I describe situations and information in precise, behavioral terms without judgments?

_____14. Do I place blame on or give advice to others? (e.g., "You should....)

_____15. Do I restate comments to assure that accurate information was understood?

After reflecting on these questions, name a communication goal for the next week.

Appendix C

RtI Organization Chart

Name of School: _____ School District:_____

District Administrator:_____ School Administrator: _____

RtI Facilitator: _____ RtI Recorder: _____

Meeting Schedule: Day: _____ Time:_____

Meeting Membership/Attendance for Semester 1:

Please check by your name for meeting attendance.

Name/Position	Sept.	Oct.	Nov.	Dec.
RtI Facilitator*				
RtI Recorder*				
Referring Teacher*				
School Administrator*				
Reading Teacher*				
School Psychologist				
Speech-Language Pathologist				
Nurse				
ESE Teacher				
Other Educator				
Other				

* denotes regular member of RtI team for this semester.

Appendix D

Response to Intervention (RtI) Implementation Planning Form

Meeting Topics:

Current Procedures-Special Education Referral Process:

_____

_____

Student Assessment (Baseline/Progress-Monitoring):

_____

_____

Intervention Planning:

_____

_____

Professional Development – Assessment and Research-based Interventions:

_____

_____

Team Planning Time

_____

_____

School-Wide RTI Coordination & Direction:

_____

_____

General Staff Questions/Issues About RTI:

_____

_____

Other:

_____

_____

Discuss Planning for Dissemination to Administrators, Faculty, Staff, and Parents.

Appendix E

RTI Team Discussion Form

Based on the RtI Meeting today, consider the following questions related to overall team functioning. After several minutes, be prepared to make suggestions for improvement.

	YES	SOME	NO
1. Did the RtI Facilitator and Recorder complete their tasks, as agreed?	1	2	3
2. Is the meeting minutes form filled out completely?	1	2	3
3. Were all the team members given an opportunity to participate?	1	2	3
4. Were the RtI members supportive of each other and the referring teacher?	1	2	3
5. Was the referring teacher supportive about the intervention plan?	1	2	3
6. Did the team use the meeting time efficiently?	1	2	3
7. Was Baseline Data on the student:			
• reviewed at the meeting?	1	2	3
• used to make decisions?	1	2	3
8. Was a clearly defined implementation and follow-up plan written?	1	2	3
9. Were the instructional and intervention plans and resources available to the classroom teacher?	1	2	3
10. Did the team determine how the intervention integrity would be monitored?	1	2	3

11. Comments:

_____

_____

Appendix F

Teacher Referral Form

Please answer the questions below so that we will be better prepared at the initial RTI meeting to talk with you about the needs of this student.

General Information

Person Making Referral: _____ Date:_____

Student Name: _____ Date of Birth: _____

Dominant Language: _____ Grade:_____

Address: _____ Phone: _____

Date parent was contacted about RTI referral:_____ By whom: _____

Medical or health concerns for this student: _____

_____

How is the student's attendance this year? _____

_____

Current school or agency support services or program(s) in place for this student (e.g., counseling, tutoring, etc.):

_____

What are several strengths, talents, or specific interests for this student?

1. _____
2. _____
3. _____

Instructional Information

What makes this student *difficult* to teach? List any academic, social, emotional, or medical factors that seem to negatively affect the student's progress. (If the problem is primarily *behavioral*, how often does the problem occur, how intense is it, and for how long does the problem last? If the problem is primarily *academic*, what specific deficits does the student have in particular academic skills or competencies?):

_____

_____

_____

Wright, J. (2007). RTI Team Teacher Referral Form (Exhibit 3B). *RTI toolkit: A practical guide for schools*. Port Chester, NY: National Professional Resources. Reprinted with permission.

How does this student's academic skills compare to those of "average" children in your classroom? (e.g., How does the student compare to peers in reading, math, writing, and organizational skills?):

_____

What is this child's estimated current reading level?

_____

List any other general information about the student's academic levels or abilities (e.g., test results) that may shed light on your referral concern:

_____

_____

Problem-Identification Information

Interventions attempted: Please describe specific attempts that you or others have made this year to meet this student's academic, social, and/or emotional needs:

Intervention	Dates Began-Ended (Approximate)	Person(s) Responsible	Outcome

If the referral concern is in academics, how much time during the period/day does the student receive instruction in the area(s) of difficulty?

_____

When have you observed the problem occurring the most? _____

Are there settings or situations in which the problem is *less* severe or *minimized*? If so, when? _____

Please list members of your instructional team/building staff whom you would like:

- To receive an invitation to the initial RTI meeting:
- To receive a copy of the RTI Intervention Plan(s) after the initial meeting:

_____   _____

What would be the best day(s)/time(s) for a member of the RTI team to observe the student having the difficulties that you describe above? (Please attach a copy of the student's daily schedule, if available):

_____

Appendix G

Anticipation Guide

An anticipation guides is a series of statements that is connected to a certain text. The use of an anticipation guide can activate prior knowledge and allow the reader to make predictions about the text.

<u>Directions</u>: Each of the following statements is connected to the content in this guide. Before reading, specify whether you agree or disagree with each statement. In addition, provide an explanation of your opinion. Consider the statements as you read and specify your level of agreement once you have finished reading the guide.

1. _____ Educators should follow the steps of instructional problem-solving in a linear fashion. Explanation:
2. _____ One piece of data can provide teachers with enough information needed to identify the specific needs of a particular student or group of students. Explanation:
3. _____ In order to get the most benefits from problem-solving, educators should have a working knowledge of statistics. Explanation:
4. _____ An educator has completed the process once all steps have been implemented. Explanation:
5. _____ Most educators participate in classroom instructional problem-solving to some degree. Explanation:
6. _____ Because classroom instructional problem-solving involves the collection of data, it alleviates the need by educators to make educated guesses regarding student learning. Explanation:
7. _____ Engaging in classroom instructional problem-solving encourages educators to assess and reflect on the effectiveness of their teaching practices. Explanation:

Kelly, M., & Rawlinson, D. (2003). *Action Research*. Tallahassee: Florida Department of Education. Adapted with permission.

Appendix H

Reading Informal Assessment:
Phonemic Segmentation

Student's Name:_____ Date:_____

Student's Score: _____ MASTERED   REMEDIATE

Directions: This test should be administered individually to students. The teacher could introduce the test by saying, "I am going to say a word; I want you to tell me all of the sounds that you hear in that word."

Practice Items: Help the student identify how to segment phonemes in a word with the following practice item. Create additional practice items as needed.

"DIM, I hear the sounds /d/ /i/ /m/."

Test Items: Read each word and allow the student to respond. Mark those items that the student answers correctly. Create additional lists as needed.

1. in	/i/ /n/	_____	(2)
2. at	/a/ /t/	_____	(2)
3. name	/n/ /ae/ /m/	_____	(3)
4. ship	/sh/ /i/ /p/	_____	(3)
5. sock	/s/ /o/ /k/	_____	(3)
6. chin	/ch/ /i/ /n/	_____	(3)
7. sand	/s/ /a/ /n/ /d/	_____	(4)

Number correct   _____

Total possible   _____ (20)

Florida Department of Education (2004). *Improving student learning through classroom action research.* Tallahassee, FL: Author. Reprinted with permission.

Appendix I

Reading Informal Assessment: Phonological Awareness

Student's Name:_____ Date:_____

Student's Score: _____ MASTERED   REMEDIATE

Directions: This test should be administered individually to students. The teacher could introduce the test by saying, "I am going to say a word and then have you say that word without one of the sounds."

Practice Items: Help the student identify how to delete phonemes in a word by using the following practice item. Create additional practice items as needed.

"Say GOAT. Now say it again without the /t/." (go)

Test Items: Read each item and allow the student to respond. Mark those items that the student answers correctly. Create additional lists as needed.

1. Say ROSE, now say it again without /z/ _____ (row)

2. Say TRAIN, now say it again without /n/ _____ (tray)

3. Say GROUP, now say it again without /p/ _____ (grew)

4. Say SEAT, now say it again without /t/ _____ (sea)

5. Say BAKE, now say it again without /k/ _____ (bay)

6. Say INCH, now say it again without /ch/ _____ (in)

7. Say SMILE, now say it again without /s/ _____ (mile)

8. Say FEET, now say it again without /f/ _____ (eat)

9. Say BOAT, now say it again without /b/ _____ (oat)

10. Say LAKE, now say it again without /l/ _____ (ache)

Number correct _____

Total possible _____

Florida Department of Education (2004). *Improving student learning through classroom action research.* Tallahassee, FL: Author. Reprinted with permission.

Appendix J

Reading Informal Assessment: Phonics Survey

Student's Name:_____ Date:_____

Student's Score: _____ MASTERED   REMEDIATE

Directions: This test should be administered individually to students. Provide the student with the Student's Copy of the Phonics Survey. The following numbers correspond with the fourteen phonics survey sections. The teacher can say the following for each skill:

1. "Can you tell me the **sound** each letter makes?"
2. "Can you tell me the **sound** each pair of letters make?"
3. "Can you tell me the **sounds** of these letters?" If the student names the letter, the teacher can say, "That is one sound, can you tell me another sound that letter makes?"
4. "Can you tell me the **names** of these letters?"
5. "Can you tell me the **names** of these letters?"
   Special note for items 6-11 – If the student cannot read more than two of the "real" words in the row, do not administer the nonsense (pseudo) row of words. Before asking the student to read the nonsense (pseudo) words the teacher can say, "Now, I will ask you to read some made up or silly words. Do not try to make them sound like real words."
6. Have the student read both rows of real and nonsense (pseudo) words.
7. Have the student read both rows of real and nonsense (pseudo) words.
8. Have the student read both rows of real and nonsense (pseudo) words.
9. Have the student read both rows of real and nonsense (pseudo) words.
10. Have the student read the rows of words.
11. Have the student read both rows of real and nonsense (pseudo) words.
12. Have the student read the row of words.
13. Have the student read the row of words.
14. Have the student read both rows of words.

Test Items: Mark those items that the student answers correctly (see Teacher and Student Copy).

Scoring: Count the number of correct responses for each skill and write it at the end of each section on the Teacher's Copy. Calculate the total correct for each skill and enter it in the corresponding box under "student's score" on the table. Mark those skills that were mastered. Create a plan for remediation as needed.

Florida Department of Education (2004). *Improving student learning through classroom action research.* Tallahassee, FL: Author. Reprinted with permission.

Reading Informal Assessment: Phonics Survey

Teacher's Copy

Name:_____ Date:_____

1. **Consonant Sounds**

m	s	f	l	r	n	h	v	w	z	c	
b	c	d	p	t	j	g	k	y	x		/21

2. **Consonant Digraphs**

sh	ch	th	ck	qu	/5

3. **Vowel Sounds**

i	e	a	o	u	/5

4. **Capital Letter Names**

B	A	I	S	C	D	F	E	P	
L	R	Z	J	U	H	G	W	X	
V	Y	N	O	K	M	T	Q		/26

5. **Lowercase Letter Names**

r	o	n	l	m	y	t	v	k	p	z	
c	d	p	t	j	g	k	b	x	q		/21

6. **Short Vowel Sounds**

hit	pot	but	mat	let	(real)	/5
fip	saf	vem	rup	wog	(nonsense)	/5

7. **Short Vowel Sounds with Consonant Digraphs**

chip	then	match	shop	luck	(real)	/5
shum	gick	chot	thap	vetch	(nonsense)	/5

8. **Short Vowel Sounds with Consonant Blends**

stop	trip	clap	dress	truck	(real)	/5
glod	stram	frip	cruz	plek	(nonsense)	/5

9. **Vowel + e**

fade	joke	mile	keep	tune	(real)	/5
leem	rafe	cude	gove	hine	(nonsense)	/5

10. **Vowel Diphthongs & Digraphs**

paid	boat	toy	root	few	
bay	saw	row	meat	high	
foot	boil	weight	suit	found	
head	glue	cry	tie	eye	/20

11. **R- and L- Controlled**

dirt	smart	bold	corn	turn	(real)	/5
burk	flar	zorp	mirt	rolt	(nonsense)	/5

12. **Prefixes**
    under   inside   replay   exit   dislike   /5

13. **Suffixes**
    sitting   nation   closest   careful   nearly   /5

14. **Multisyllabic Words**
    cupcake   bookmark   combination
    calculate   entertain   refreshment   /6

Phonics Skill	Student's Score	Possible Score	Skills Mastered
Consonant Sounds		21	
Consonant Digraphs		21	
Vowel Sounds		5	
Capital Letter Names		26	
Lower Case Letter Names		21	
Reading and Phonetic Decoding			
Short Vowel Sound		10	
Short Vowel with Consonant Digraph		10	
Short Vowel with Consonant Blends		10	
Vowel + e		10	
Vowel Diphthongs		20	
R- and L- Controlled		10	
Prefixes		5	
Suffixes		5	
Multi-Syllabic words		6	

Appendix K

Classroom Problem Identification

Reflect on and complete the following open-ended probes to assist you in investigating your initial concerns and identifying a classroom problem or area of concern.

Currently in my classroom, I am concerned about:

In order to investigate my concern, I need to collect information on:

I will gather this information by collecting the following sources of data :

After analyzing my data, I found that my students are having difficulties with:

To meet my students' needs, I need to focus my instruction on:

Florida Department of Education (2004). *Improving student learning through classroom action research.* Tallahassee, FL: Author. Reprinted with permission.

Example Chart: Classroom Problem Identification

Name: Mrs. Lue (3rd grade teacher) and Ms. Robinson (ESE coteacher)

Currently in my classroom, I am concerned about:
  Donny and Julie, two of our third graders with specific learning disabilities, are having difficulties reading and writing independently. They entered the 3rd grade reading instructionally at the pre-primer level. On the 3rd grade writing rubrics, Donny and Julie consistently scored Level 1, which is the lowest level of performance.
  Donny refuses to attempt any writing or reading assignment. He shuts down when asked to engage in any of these assignments. Being the beginning of the school year, we reviewed his cumulative records and found that he has made very little progress in reading and writing.
  Julie will attempt to read and write initially, but often gets frustrated and demands continuous support or behavior problems will occur. Her writing is very immature and will rewrite the same message every day regardless of the writing prompt or topic.

In order to investigate my concern, I need to collect information on:
  We need to investigate why Donny and Julie are not reading and writing by assessing their reading readiness skills such as their knowledge of letters and sounds, sight words, phonemic awareness abilities, and knowledge of phonics.

I will gather this information by collecting the following sources of data :
  In addition to the reading and writing assessments currently used, we will gather more information through the following informal assessment surveys focusing on letter identification, letter/sound correspondence, phonemic awareness, phonics, and sight words.

After analyzing my data, I found that my students are having difficulties with:
  After analyzing the various assessments, we found that Donny and Julie both have poor letter sounds correspondence, weak phonemic awareness, a limited repertoire of sight words, and a lack of reading and writing strategies.
  Donny was unable to identify letters of the alphabet and produce sounds to the letters. Furthermore, the only sight words in his current vocabulary were "Donny", "I", and "a".
  It seems that Julie continuously wrote the same message because those were the only words in her sight vocabulary. She too had significant difficulties with letter sound correspondence and struggled with hearing and recording sounds in words.

To meet my students' needs, I need to focus my instruction on:
  Donny and Julie will require instruction specifically designed to target building letter/sound correspondence, phonemic awareness, and phonics in a comprehensive approaching connecting reading to writing.

Appendix L

Classroom Environment Inventory

1. Describe your classroom set-up and student seating arrangement. Identify distracters:

2. What are the classroom rules?

3. What are the consequences for breaking classroom rules?

4. How do you handle student conflict and/or discipline issues?

5. What instructional methods do you use?

6. What does a class period generally consist of?

7. How do you work with students in your classroom?

8. What are students required to do in your class?

9. What materials and supplies are needed by students? Are the instructional resources evidence-based? Do you have intervention materials?

10. What additional interventions or accommodations do you use generally?

Appendix M

Identifying a Classroom Problem

Name(s):

School:

Grade Level:

Problem Statement: Compose a problem statement specifically describing <u>who is affected</u>, <u>supported causes of the problem</u>, the <u>goal for improvement</u>, and <u>what might be done about the problem</u> as stated. (Provide as much specific information as possible).

Completed Example Chart: Identifying a Classroom Problem

Name(s): *Mrs. Lue and Ms. Robinson*

School: *ABC Elementary School*

Grade Level: *3rd Grade, Language Arts (Inclusive Classroom)*

Problem Statement: Compose a problem statement specifically describing who is affected, supported causes of the problem, the goal for improvement, and what might be done about the problem as stated. (Provide as much specific information as possible.)

Two of our third grade students with specific learning disabilities and language impairments are having difficulty learning to read and write. They entered third grade reading instructionally at the pre-primer level and consistently scoring a Level 1 on their writing rubrics. After further investigation, we found that Donny and Julie have poor letter/sound correspondence, weak phonemic awareness and phonics, and a limited repertoire of sight words. Our goal for these two students is to build their letter sound correspondence while improving their ability to hear and record sounds in words. In addition to their regular reading and writing instruction, Donny and Julie will receive small group instruction geared to meeting their goal for improvement.

Appendix N

Classroom Instructional Problem-Solving Plan

Name(s):   **School:**   **Grade Level:**

Research Question: Pose a question that will focus your study. Be sure to include what student learning will occur and what instructional practices will be implemented.

Learning Outcomes: What specific student learning will occur?

Instructional Focus: Describe the specific instructional practice(s) that will be implemented and studied. Specify when and how the practice will be implemented.

Data Collection: Specify the data sources that you will collect that are aligned to the classroom problem. Describe how often will you collect the data?

Data Source 1: (What & How?)

Data Source 2: (What & How?)

Data Source 3: (What & How?)

Support: What support will you need from your colleagues?

Florida Department of Education (2004). *Improving student learning through classroom action research.* Tallahassee, FL: Author. Reprinted with permission.

Example: Classroom Instructional Problem-solving Plan

Name(s): *Mrs. Lue & Ms. Robinson*
School: *ABC Elementary School*
Grade Level: *3rd Grade*

Research Question: Pose a question that will focus your study. Be sure to include what student learning will occur and what instructional practices will be implemented.

How will incorporating visible prompts and hands-on manipulatives into small group reading instruction affect my students' ability to hear and record sounds in words and increase the identified sight words?

Learning Outcomes: What specific student learning will occur?

Donny and Julie will improve their letter/sound correspondence.

Donny and Julie will improve their ability to hear and record sounds in words (phonemic awareness and phonics).

Donny and Julie will increase the number of identified sight words.

Instructional Focus: Describe the specific instructional practice(s) that will be implemented and studied. Specify when and how the practice will be implemented.

Donny and Julie will receive small group reading instruction using a scientifically-based program and resources following a systematic instructional plan which includes daily word work that will incorporate the following teaching techniques and manipulatives:

• *Providing explicit instruction in developing letter-sound correspondence*
• *Building the ability to hear and record sounds in words by incorporating Elkonin Boxes (tokens and letters) and other visible prompts into daily word work*
• *Using letter magnets, white boards, shaving cream, chalkboard/water for practicing building and manipulating words*
• *Connecting reading to writing using a scientifically-based reading instruction program*

Data Collection: Specify the data sources that you will collect that are aligned to the classroom problem. Describe how often will you collect the data?

Data Source 1: (What & How?)
Letter-Sound Identification Survey, bi-monthly

Data Source 2: (What & How?)
Sight Word Identification and Phonics Survey, bi-monthly

Data Source 3: (What & How?)
Hearing and Recording Sounds in Words (Writing Samples, Observations), Daily

Data Source 4: (What & How?)
School required reading and writing assessments, every 9 weeks

Support: What support will you need from your colleagues?
• Coaching and guidance from our Literacy Coach

Appendix O

Implementation Schedule

Tasks	Timeline Beginning/Ending	Resources

Example of Completed Implementation Schedule

Tasks	Timeline Beginning/Ending	Resources
Investigate area of concern by administering informal assessment	9/1 –9/5	Informal assessment surveys
Analyze informal assessments	9/8	Time and planning period
Consult with Literacy Coach for developing instructional focus	9/10	Analyzed informal assessments, time, and planning period
Locate materials for reading instruction	9/12 – 9/15	Resource Teacher, Literacy Coach Manipulatives, and books
Implement instructional focus	9/02 – 2/03	Reading materials, manipulatives, and resources
Monitor students' learning	9/02 – 2/03 daily, bi-monthly, and every nine weeks	Informal assessments, school required assessments, time for analysis, and planning period
Follow-up meeting	10/02	Time for analyses of continuous progress monitoring data to evaluate impact of planning

Appendix P

Essential Task List for Fidelity of Implementation

Directions: In the second column, write the name of the individual or team who will assume responsibility for the task identified in the first column. In the third column, write the deadline for completion of the task and/or status when reviewed.

Task	Individual / Team	Timeline/Status
Develop a system of professional development and training as the school begins RtI implementation and as it hires new staff.		
Develop a fidelity data collection system that includes both direct (e.g., checklists) and indirect (e.g., permanent products) measures.		
Develop criteria (i.e., parent accuracy) to indicate when a teacher may need additional supports.		
Coordinate master schedules to conduct fidelity checks (i.e., teacher evaluations, walk-through checks, trainings).		
Develop a plan to systematically review results of fidelity information collected.		
Develop a plan to provide additional supports and professional development.		

National Research Center on Learning Disabilities (2006). *Core concepts of RtI.* Retrieved July 25, 2007, from www.nrcld.org

Appendix Q

Observations: Anecdotal Records
Name of student(s)
Date:
Date:
Date:
Date:

Appendix R

Observation Recording Table
Small Group or Class

Date: Objective:				
Name:	Name:	Name:	Name:	Name:
Name:	Name:	Name:	Name:	Name:
Name:	Name:	Name:	Name:	Name:

Appendix S

Interval and Time Sampling Observation Sheet

Teacher _____ Student _____ Grade _____

Observer _____ Time Started _____ Time Ended _____

Behavior _____ Activity _____ Date _____

Recording Codes: + = Occurrence   Baseline_____ Intervention_____
                     O = Nonoccurrence

                                            Observation Intervals: 10   20   30
                                                                        (seconds)

Appendix T

Writing Continuum Checklist

Preconventional

Making marks other than drawing on paper (scribble writing)
Primarily relies on pictures to convey meaning
Sometimes labels and adds "words" to pictures
Tells about own writing

Emergent

Sees self as writer
Copies names and familiar words
Uses pictures and print to convey meaning
Pretends to read own writing
Prints with upper-case letters
Uses beginning/ending consonants to make words

Developing

Takes risks with writing
Begins to read own writing
Writes names and favorite words
Writing is from top-bottom left-right front-back
May interchange upper and lower-case letters
Uses beginning, middle, and ending sounds to make words
Begins to write noun-verb phrases

Beginning

Writes pieces that self and others can read
Begins to write recognizable short sentences
Writes about observations and experiences with some
    descriptive words
Experiments with capitals and punctuation
Forms many letters legibly
Uses phonetics spelling to write independently
Spells some words correctly
Begins to revise by adding on

Expanding

Begins to consider audience
Writes pieces with beginning, middle, and end
Revises by adding description and detail
Listens to peer's writing and offers feedback
Edits for punctuation and spelling
Uses capital letters and periods
Forms letters with ease
Spelling many common words correctly

Appendix U

Student Record Form: Curriculum-Based Measurement, Oral Reading Fluency

Student Name: _____ Grade/Classroom: _____

Reading Skill Level:_____ Best Time(s) for CBM Monitoring: _____

Step 1: Conduct a Survey-Level Assessment: Use this section to record the student's reading rates in progressively more difficult material.

Date:_____ Book/Reading Level:_____

	TRW	E	CRW	%CRW
A.	____	____	____	____
B.	____	____	____	____
C.	____	____	____	____

Date:_____ Book/Reading Level:_____

	TRW	E	CRW	%CRW
A.	____	____	____	____
B.	____	____	____	____
C.	____	____	____	____

Date:_____ Book/Reading Level:_____

	TRW	E	CRW	%CRW
A.	____	____	____	____
B.	____	____	____	____
C.	____	____	____	____

Date:_____ Book/Reading Level:_____

	TRW	E	CRW	%CRW
A.	____	____	____	____
B.	____	____	____	____
C.	____	____	____	____

Date:_____ Book/Reading Level:_____

	TRW	E	CRW	%CRW
A.	____	____	____	____
B.	____	____	____	____
C.	____	____	____	____

Date:_____ Book/Reading Level:_____

	TRW	E	CRW	%CRW
A.	____	____	____	____
B.	____	____	____	____
C.	____	____	____	____

Date:_____ Book/Reading Level:_____

	TRW	E	CRW	%CRW
A.	____	____	____	____
B.	____	____	____	____
C.	____	____	____	____

Table 1: Sample Estimates of "Typical" CBM Instructional Reading Levels by Grade

	Shapiro (1996)		Milwaukee Public Schools (Winter 2000-2001 Local Norms)
	CRW Per Min	Reading Errors	CRW Per Min for Students in 25th-75th Percentile
Grade			
1	40-60	Fewer than 5	22-64
2	40-60	Fewer than 5	36-78
3	70-100	Fewer than 7	47-88
4	70-100	Fewer than 7	60-104
5	70-100	Fewer than 7	77-121
6	70-100	Fewer than 7	95-146

Step 2: Compute a Student Reading Goal
1. At what grade or book level will the student be monitored? (Refer to results of Step 1: Survey-Level Assessment)_____
2. What is the student's baseline reading rate (# correctly read words per min)? ____ CRW Per Min
3. When is the start date to begin monitoring the student in reading? ____/____/____.
4. When is the end date to begin monitoring the student in reading? ____/____/____.
5. How many instructional weeks are there between the start and end dates? (Round to the nearest week if necessary): _____ Instructional Weeks
6. What do you predict the student's average increase in correctly read words per minute will be for each instructional week of the monitoring period? (see table 2):
7. What will the student's predicted CRW gain in reading fluency be at the end of monitoring? (Multiply Item 5 by 6): _____.
8. What will the student's predicted reading rate be at the end of the monitoring period? (add items 2 & &): _____CRW Per Min.

Step 3: Collect Baseline Data: Give 3 CBM reading assessments within a one-week period using monitoring-level probes.

Date:_____ Book/Reading Level:_____

	TRW	E	CRW	%CRW
A.	_____	_____	_____	_____
B.	_____	_____	_____	_____
C.	_____	_____	_____	_____

Date:_____ Book/Reading Level:_____

	TRW	E	CRW	%CRW
A.	_____	_____	_____	_____
B.	_____	_____	_____	_____
C.	_____	_____	_____	_____

Date:_____ Book/Reading Level:_____

	TRW	E	CRW	%CRW
A.	_____	_____	_____	_____
B.	_____	_____	_____	_____
C.	_____	_____	_____	_____

Step 4: Complete CBM Progress-Monitoring Weekly or More Frequency: Record the results of regular monitoring of the student's progress in reading fluency.

Date:_____ Book/Reading Level:_____

	TRW	E	CRW	%CRW
A.	_____	_____	_____	_____
B.	_____	_____	_____	_____
C.	_____	_____	_____	_____

Date:_____ Book/Reading Level:_____

	TRW	E	CRW	%CRW
A.	_____	_____	_____	_____
B.	_____	_____	_____	_____
C.	_____	_____	_____	_____

Date:_____ Book/Reading Level:_____

	TRW	E	CRW	%CRW
A.	_____	_____	_____	_____
B.	_____	_____	_____	_____
C.	_____	_____	_____	_____

Date:_____ Book/Reading Level:_____

	TRW	E	CRW	%CRW
A.	_____	_____	_____	_____
B.	_____	_____	_____	_____
C.	_____	_____	_____	_____

Date:_____ Book/Reading Level:_____

	TRW	E	CRW	%CRW
A.	_____	_____	_____	_____
B.	_____	_____	_____	_____
C.	_____	_____	_____	_____

	TRW	E	CRW	%CRW
A.	_____	_____	_____	_____
B.	_____	_____	_____	_____
C.	_____	_____	_____	_____

Date:_____ Book/Reading Level:_____

	TRW	E	CRW	%CRW
A.	_____	_____	_____	_____
B.	_____	_____	_____	_____
C.	_____	_____	_____	_____

Date:_____ Book/Reading Level:_____

	TRW	E	CRW	%CRW
A.	_____	_____	_____	_____
B.	_____	_____	_____	_____
C.	_____	_____	_____	_____

Date:_____ Book/Reading Level:_____

	TRW	E	CRW	%CRW
A.	_____	_____	_____	_____
B.	_____	_____	_____	_____
C.	_____	_____	_____	_____

Date:_____ Book/Reading Level:_____

	TRW	E	CRW	%CRW
A.	_____	_____	_____	_____
B.	_____	_____	_____	_____
C.	_____	_____	_____	_____

Date:_____ Book/Reading Level:_____

	TRW	E	CRW	%CRW
A.	_____	_____	_____	_____
B.	_____	_____	_____	_____
C.	_____	_____	_____	_____

Date:_____ Book/Reading Level:_____

	TRW	E	CRW	%CRW
A.	_____	_____	_____	_____
B.	_____	_____	_____	_____
C.	_____	_____	_____	_____

Table 2: Predictions for Rates of Reading Growth by Grade (Fuchs, Fuchs, Hamlett, Walz, & Germann, 1993). Increase in correctly read words per minute for each instructional week.

Grade Level		Realistic Weekly Goal	Ambitious Weekly Goal
Grade 1		2.0	3.0
Grade 2		1.5	2.0
Grade 3		1.0	1.5
Grade 4		0.85	1.1
Grade 5		0.5	0.8
Grade 6		0.3	0.65

Appendix V

Student Interview: Learning Survey

Student Name:_____ Classroom: _____ Date: _____

Directions: Please complete this survey about how you learn best. If you are not sure what to put for an answer, just write down your "best guess".

1. What do you prefer to be called by your teacher? _____

2. When is your birthday? _____

3. What is your most favorite subject or school activity? _____

4. What is you least favorite subject or school activity? _____

5. Do you like working in groups or alone on projects?

    State your reason(s) why: _____

6. Organizational skills include having all of your work materials on hand in the classroom, using your work time well, and getting work assignments done and handed in on time. ON a rating scale from 1 (the lowest rating) to 10 (the highest rating), how would you rate your organizational sills?

        1   2   3   4   5   6   7   8   9   10
    Not organized at all   Very organized

7. Describe your idea of the perfect classroom. What would it look like?

    _____

    _____

8. What are your favorite ways to learn? (pick as many as you like)
    ___ Listening to lectures   ___ Working with a friend
    ___ Working as part of a group   ___ Listening to a taped book
    ___ Doing homework   ___ Doing research in libraries
    ___ Doing research on the internet ___ Watching an educational video
    ___ Other: _____

9. Write two words that best describes you:

    _____

10. What are your favorite games, activities, sports, hobbies, or other interests?

_____

_____

11. What are your favorite TV shows or movies?

_____

_____

12. Describe how you study or review for a test:

_____

_____

13. Occasionally, students can earn rewards in the class for working hard and tru-ing in completed work. What would be some good rewards or privileges you would like to be able to earn in this classroom? (Be realistic!):

_____

_____

_____

Reading at Home

Interview

Name:

Date:

1. How many minutes a day do you spend reading books at home?

2. When is your favorite time to read?

3. What is your favorite book to read? What is your favorite topic to read about?

4. What was the last book that you read?

5. When do your parents read to you at home?

6. How does reading make you feel?

Appendix W

Identifying Language and Reading Needs & Instructional Planning

Student Name: _____ Grade: _____

Date of Plan: _____ Date of RtI Meeting: _____

Teacher: _____ Speech Language Pathologist:_____

Reading Coach: _____ School Psychologist: _____

Other:_____

School-Based Assessments and Classroom Screening Results		What reading diagnostic(s) were administered and analyzed?	Instructional Planning, Progress Monitoring, and Monitoring Instruction	
School Based Assessment Results	What do we know?	Name of diagnostic(s):	Reading Component(s)	Target Skills:
Classroom Screening Results		Results:	Learning Outcome(s):	Strategy/ Intervention:
Core Instruction and Results	What do we need to know?	Student's strengths and needs:	Instruction Timeline	Progress Monitoring
		Strengths: Needs:		

Appendix X

Sharing Problem-Solving Results: Sample Report

Sample Report of Interventions in Phonological Awareness Results of Phonological Awareness Instruction in Three Kindergarten Classrooms

Introduction

Phonological awareness is the ability to notice, think about, and manipulate the individual sounds in words (Blackman et al, 1999; Foorman, Francis, Fletcher, Schatschneider, & Mehta, 1998)). For example, the word "cat" has three sounds, or phonemes, /k//a//t/. These three sounds can be manipulated in several ways. They can be isolated into their component phonemes (segmentation). One phoneme could be substituted for another, changing the word (e.g., changing the middle phoneme to /o/ which gives you the word "cot"). One can rhyme "cat" with "fat" or "rat," or isolate the initial phoneme, /c/ from /at/, or blend the three phonemes together to make the word "cat."

In spoken language, we do not need to attend to or even be aware of individual phonemes to process complex phonological information (Torgesen & Mathes, 1999). In the above example, when we say or hear the word "cat," the three separate phonemes overlap into one sound. The process of hearing and understanding speech is a natural one. However, reading is not a natural process. Our natural approach to speech may actually interfere with beginning reading. Spoken words are heard and processed as one sound, but the beginning reader must learn to identify the smallest units of language, phonemes, to be successful in learning which sounds go with which letters (Lyon, 1998). Therefore, phonological awareness is essential for success in beginning reading acquisition.

Phonological awareness, like reading, often needs to be taught explicitly. About 25% of students from middle-class homes will not acquire phonological awareness by first grade unless they are provided with direct instructional support. This percentage increases substantially (Wagner et al, 1997). Furthermore, children with low phonological awareness often have serious difficulties in leaning to read and write. The level of phonological awareness on entering school is the greatest single predictor of a student's success in learning how to read (O'Connor et al, 2005).

Three different schools volunteered one kindergarten classroom for the study, and collectively the three classrooms became the experimental group. A fourth kindergarten classroom, which served as the control group, was located at one of the three participating schools. Class sizes ranged from 20 to 24 students. The purpose of this action research was to assess the effectiveness of phonological awareness instruction in three kindergarten classrooms. Procedures

To get an initial idea of the children's phonological awareness skills, all students were given a screening instrument prior to receiving any instruction. The instrument used is described below under Measures.

Each teacher was trained to use the Phonemic Awareness in Young Children curriculum (Adams, Foorman, Lundberg, & Beeler, 1998b). The teacher teamed up with the speech/language specialist at her school and taught lessons to her entire class approximately 15 minutes per day, 2-3 days per week.

In January, all children were assessed again with the screening instrument. Students who appeared to make little progress were pulled out for small-group instruction with the speech/language specialist. This small-group instruction occurred at least 2 times per week for 20 minutes each time, and group sizes ranged from 4 to 8 students. The speech/language specialists used The Phonological Awareness Kit (Robertson & Salter, 1995a) for the small-group instruction while the classroom teachers continued to teach phonemic awareness to the entire class using the Phonemic Awareness in Young Children curriculum. In May all students were assessed again using the screening instrument.

Although procedures had been outlined for the three pilot classrooms, the implementation varied among classrooms. For example, Pilot Classroom I implemented whole-group instruction daily for 15 minutes and the small-group instruction was conducted 4 times per week for 25 minutes each. Pilot Classrooms 2 and 3 implemented whole-group instruction 2-3 times per week for 15 minutes each, and small-group instruction occurred 2 times per week from 20-30 minutes per session.

Students in the control classroom did not receive any explicit instruction in phonological awareness. They were assessed in January and May with the screening instrument, but the information was not used by school staff. It was collected for the sole purpose of comparison to the experimental group.

Student performance was assessed using The Phonological Awareness Profile (Robertson & Salter, 1995b). This measure assesses phonological awareness skills in six areas: rhyming (10 items), segmentation (25 items), isolation (15 items), deletion (15 items), substitution (10 items), and blending (10 items). All items are administered unless the student answers 3 consecutive items on a subtask incorrectly. The measure takes approximately 20 minutes to administer. For this project, the assessment was performed by the speech/language specialist who was working with the students.

Results

To assess the effects of the phonological awareness activities on student acquisition of phonological awareness skills, total raw scores on the Phonological Awareness Profile administered in January and May were examined in two ways. The first set of analyses examined the data according to whether phonemic awareness was taught. The three pilot classrooms were compared collectively to the control classroom. The second set of analyses examined the differences between the four classrooms involved in the project.

Results from the first analysis are summarized below:

Table 1. Mean Scores on Phonological Awareness Profile in January and May by Condition

Condition	January	May
Pilot Classrooms	37.2(8.6)	45.7(6.5)
Control Classroom	34.5(9.6)	39.5(7.8)

Note. Standard Deviations are in parentheses. Maximum score = 55.

Analysis of variance conducted on the January scores show no significant differences between conditions, $f(1,86) = 1.55$, $p>.05$. That is, the students involved in the pilot project did not have significantly higher scores in January than students in the control classroom.

Analysis of covariance conducted on the May scores, using the January scores as the covariate, revealed a significant difference between conditions $F(1,86) = 7.20$, $p<05$. The effect size associated with this difference is .85. That is, in May the students in the pilot classrooms scored .85 standard deviation units higher than students in the control classroom.

Because implementation of the phonological awareness activities was not uniform across the three classrooms, a second analysis was performed to examine differences in outcomes by classrooms. Results from this second analysis are summarized below:

Table 2. Mean Scores on Phonological Awareness Profile in January and May by Classroom

Classroom	January	May
Pilot Classroom #1	40.0(8.9)	49.5(5.9)
Pilot Classroom #2	32.5(8.8)	42.0(5.8)
Pilot Classroom #3	38.6(6.4)	44.7(5.5)
Control Classroom	34.5(9.6)	39.5(8.0)

Note. Standard deviations are in parentheses. Maximum score = 55.

Analysis of variance conducted on the January scores show significant differences between classrooms, $E(3,86) = 3.6\ 1$, $p<05$. Follow-up analyses show that Classroom 1 scores were higher than Classroom 2 scores, but no other differences are significant.

Analysis of covariance conducted on the May scores, using the January scores as the covariate, also revealed a significant difference between conditions, $f(3,86) = 4.30$, $p<05$. Follow-up analyses show that Classroom I scores were significantly higher than all other scores, and that Classroom 3 scores were significantly higher than the control group. No other differences were significant.

Discussion

The purpose of this action research project was to examine the effectiveness of phonological awareness instruction in kindergarten classrooms. Three kindergarten teachers worked with their speech/language specialist to provide whole-class instruction 2-5 times per week, and small-group instruction 2-4 times per week. Teachers and speech/language specialists used packaged curricula and assessment measures. Overall, students in the pilot classrooms showed greater gains in phonological awareness skills than students in the control classroom. Further, students in the classroom whose teacher and speech/language specialist implemented the most instruction had the highest levels of phonological awareness skills by the end of the year. These findings support the notion that phonological awareness instruction can be successfully implemented in kindergarten classrooms.

Appendix Y

Sharing Your Results: Reporting Format

Name of Teacher Researcher:

Name of School and County:

<u>Research Site</u>: *Provide a description of your school site. Details may include demographic information, number of students, grade level, specific programs or instructional methods being implemented, etc.*

<u>Teacher Researcher(s)</u>: *Describe what grade level and content you are currently teaching. Provide information on specific professional development activities that focus on the stated instructional concern.*

<u>Problem:</u> *Provide a description of your identified classroom problem. How did you identify the classroom problem? Describe the students who were affected and possible causes of the problem. What were the goals for improvement?*

<u>Research Process</u>: *Provide a detailed description of your research process. What was your research question? What instructional strategies or practices were implemented that were aligned to the classroom problem? Describe your implementation.*

<u>Data Analysis:</u> *Provide a narrative summary of your collected and analyzed data. If appropriate, please include graphs and tables to accompany the narrative summary. Include templates of your data collection sources as well as student samples.*

<u>Taking Action:</u> *Provide a summary of your decisions based on your analyzed data. What are your next steps? Do you need to continue your plan using the same procedures? Do you need to revise your procedures? Were you satisfied with your results and ready to investigate new concerns?*

<u>Professional Reflection:</u> *What did you learn through this process? How did this process impact your teaching?*

Appendix Z

Classroom Instructional Problem-solving, Pre- and Post-tests

1. In your own words, define Classroom Instructional Problem-solving.

2. In which areas in the educational setting could you apply Classroom Instructional Problem-solving?

3. Describe the process of Classroom Instructional Problem-solving.

4. Discuss several ways of collecting data.

5. Why is triangulating data an important practice in Classroom Instructional Problem-solving?

6. Identify several ways of sharing Classroom Instructional Problem-solving results.

7. Why is Classroom Instructional Problem-solving valuable to students, class-room teachers, and schools?

Resources

For more information, contact the Regional Resource Center in your area.

Web addresses from the U.S. Regional Resource Centers.

Northeast Regional Resource Center (NERRC)	http://www.rrfcnetwork.org/NERRC/
Mid-South Regional Resource Center (MSRRC)	http://www.rrfcnetwork.org/MSRRC/
Southeast Regional Resource Center (SERRC)	http://www.rrfcnetwork.org/SERRC.
Great Lakes Area Regional Resource Center (GLARRC)	http://www.csnp.ohio-state.edu/glarrc.htm
Mountain Plains Regional Resource Center (MPRRC)	http://www.rrfcnetwork.org/MPRRC/
Western Regional Resource Center (WRRC)	http://www.rrfcnetwork.org/wrrc/

Websites

Response to Intervention Resources

http://www.nrcld.org/

This website of the National Research Center of Learning Disabilities (NCLD) includes numerous resources (professional papers, presentations, etc.) written to provide guidance and information to the developing Response to Intervention initiative.

http://www.ncld/org/images/stories/downloads/parent_center/rti_final.pdf

NCLD has written a parent's guide to Response to Intervention to provide an overview of the RtI process, describe how it is implemented in schools, and offers questions and answers for parents.

http://iris.peabody.vanderbilt.edu/rti/chalcycle.htm

These online modules provide information on Response to Intervention. The modules include information on awareness, eligibility, models, and procedures in an interactive format.

http://www.studentprogress.org

To meet the challenges of implementing effective progress monitoring, the Office of Special Education Programs (OSEP) has funded the National Center on Student Progress monitoring. Housed at the American Institutes for Research, and working in conjunction with researchers from Vanderbilt University, the National Center on Student Progress Monitoring provides technical assistance to states and districts in various monitoring practices proven to work in different content areas in Grades 1-5.

http://www.k8accesscenter.org

The Access Center is a national technical assistance center funded by the US Department of Education's Office of Special Education Programs. Its mission is to improve educational outcomes for elementary and middle school students with disabilities. They are dedicated to building capacity of TA systems, states, districts, and schools.

Professional Organization Websites

The topics of RtI, action research, instructional problem-solving, and student progress monitoring are included on the websites of numerous professional organizations including:

Council for Exceptional Children	http://www.cec.sped.org
Association for School Psychologists	http://nasponline.org
American Speech-Language-Hearing Association	http://www.asha.org
School Social Work Association	http://www.sswaa.org
National Association of State Directors	http://nasdse.org
International Reading Association	http://reading.org

Online Reading and Literacy Assessment Resources

http://teachers.henric.k12.va.us/Specialist/franceslively/reading.htm

This website presents reading resources for teachers such as free reading assessments, reading aptitude assessments tests, activities for lesson plan development, and links to various online resources: graphic organizers, educational reference books, etc.

http://usd273.k12.ks.us/elementary/

This Beloit Elementary School website provides BES Assessment Forms & Rubrics for teachers in grades K-5. Reading Response Journal Rubrics, Speaking Rubrics, Problem-solving Rubrics, and Listening Rubrics are all reproducible.

http://www.educ.state.ak.us/tls/frameworks/langarts/42tools.htm

The Alaska Department of Education & Early Development provides sample assessment tools for teachers in Reading/Language Arts as well as other subject areas. Analytic rubrics, holistic rubrics, and samples of assessment tools used in classrooms are provided.

http://www.tea.state.tx.us/student.assessment/taks/rubrics/

The Texas Education Agency, Student Assessment Division, supplies reproducible TAKS Writing and Reading Rubrics for secondary teachers.

http://doe.state.in.us/publications/phonics.html

The State of Indiana Department of Education's Office of Program Development has posted a downloadable Phonics Toolkit for teachers. The toolkit provides sheets and strategies, suggestions, and assessment tools for teachers.

http://www.lm.havre.k12.mt.us/teachertools/tools.html

The Havre Public School system's Instructional Technology Specialist, J. Rygg, in Havre, Montana has created a website of Teacher Tools, On-Line Presentations, Internet Excursions, Internet Partnerships, and Learning Activities for teachers in the K-12 Educational Community. This site enables to teachers to link to many assessment tools (such as rubric makers), games, and activities in Reading, Writing, Math, Geography, etc.

http://intranet.cps.k12.il.us/Assessments/Ideas_and_Rubrics/
Rubric_Bank/ReadingRubrics.pdf

Chicago Public Schools Bureau of Assessment provides reproducible examples of Reading and Social Studies Rubrics from various Public School Systems across the country.

http://www.fcrr.org/assessment/pdffiles/prek_kassessments.pdf

Pre—Kindergarten and Kindergarten Emergent Literacy Skills Assessments are provided by the Florida Center for Reading Research. They are reproducible and designed to aid teachers in helping students build early literacy skills.

http://www.benchmarkschool.org/b_intro.htm

Benchmark School provides students the tools and strategies they need to become lifelong learners, thinkers, and problem-solvers. Their well researched program provides staff development opportunities for teachers working with readers and writers who struggle with language arts.

http://www.nichcy.org/resources/literacy2.asp

Connections to Literacy provides, in one place, links to the substantial research and instructional knowledge base that has emerged in recent years on reading. This resource is divided into the following sections: Research Basics, NCLB and Reading, Teaching Reading: Is it Rocket Science?, Beginning Reading Instruction, Reading with Older Children, Don't Miss Resources, Literacy and Children with Disabilities, and Reading and English Learners.

http://www.getreadytoread.org/

Getting Ready to Read is a program of the National Center for Learning Disabilities. It represents a national initiative to build early literacy skills of preschool-age children by providing parents, educators, health care-professionals, and advocates with information and tools for screening and teaching all children to read and write. The site may be accessed in both English and Spanish.

http://www.orton-gillingham.com/

Orton Gillingham Institute for Multi-Sensory Education (IMSE) offers phonetic, sequential, and success-oriented programs for teachers and parents to use to enhance children's skills in reading, spelling, and writing.

http://www.readingrockets.org/index.php

Reading Rockets is a national multimedia website offering information and resources on how people learn to read, why many experience difficulty reading, and what parents and teachers can do to help. The United States Department of Education, Office of Special Education, funds the Reading Rockets project. The site provides access in both English and Spanish to PBS programming, video tapes, books, and an extensive collection of online services for students, teachers, and parents.

http://www.alliance.brown.edu/tdl/index.shtml

Teaching Diverse Learners is a Web site dedicated to enhancing the capability of teachers to work effectively and equitably with English Language Learners (ELLs). This Web site provides access to many research based publications and materials, most of which are downloadable. Topics covered include, assessment, elementary literacy, strategies, legislative and legal policy and families.

http://www.oise.utoronto.ca/~ctd/networks/

An on-line journal for professionals involved in teacher research projects. The site offers archived research projects for review, book reviews, and discussion links for ongoing projects.

http://www.nsdc.org/educatorindex.htm

The National Staff Development Council is devoted to increasing awareness and support for staff development opportunities on a national level. The website is dedicated to providing up-to-date information about staff development research, opportunities, and information. It offers information and resources through its library link.

http://www.gse.gmu.edu/research/tr/index.shtml

> This website by George Mason University's Graduate School of Education is an extensive site covering the basics of action research, the steps in the process, and discussion of data analysis and conclusions. It also offers a growing online archive of finished action research projects.

http://teachers.henric.k12.va.us/Specialist/franceslively/reading.htm

> This website presents reading resources for teachers such as free reading assessments, reading aptitude assessments tests, activities for lesson plan development, and links to various online resources: graphic organizers, educational reference books, and the like.

References

Adams, M. J., Foorman, B., Lundverg, I., & Beeler, T. (1998). *Phonemic Awareness in Young Children: A Classroom Curriculum.* Baltimore, MD: Brookes.

Aitken, N., Glanfield, F., Joyner, N., Midgett, C., Simpson, S., & Thompson, C. (2003). *Classroom assessment for school mathematics: Mathematics assessment a practical handbook for grades k–2.* Reston, Virginia: National Council of Teachers of Mathematics.

Allen, C., Ferguson, S. K., Gadd, J., Koch, L. C., Kravin, D., Lambdin, D., & Rasmussen, M. (2001). *Classroom assessment for school mathematics: Mathematics assessment a practical handbook for grades 3–5.* Reston, Virginia: National Council of Teachers of Mathematics.

American Speech–Language–Hearing Association (2006). *Responsiveness-to-intervention technical assistance packet.* Retrieved August 20, 2007 from www.asha.org

Batsche, G., Elliott, J., Garden, J. L., Kovaleski, J. F., Prasse, D., et al. (2006). *Response to intervention: Policy considerations and implementation* (4th ed). Alexandria, VA: National Association of State Directors of Special Education.

Bender, W. N., & Shores, C. (2007). *Response to intervention: A practical guide for every teacher.* Thousand Oaks, CA: Corwin Press.

Bergan, J. R. (1977). *Behavioral consultation.* Columbus, OH: Charles E. Merrill.

Bernhardt, V. L. (1998). *Data analysis for comprehensive schoolwide improvement.* Larchmont, NY: Eye on Education.

Bradley, R., Danielson, L., & Doolittle, J. (2005). Response to intervention. *Journal of Learning Disabilities, 38* (96), 485–486.

Calhoun, E. (2002). Action research for school improvement. *Educational Leadership, 59*(6), 18–24.

Chalfant J. C., Pysh, M. V., & Moultrie, R. (1979). Teacher Assistance teams: A model of within-building problems solving. *Learning Disability Quarterly, 2*(3), 85–996.

Christ, T. J., Burns, M. K., & Ysseldyke, J. E. (2005). Conceptual confusion within response-to-intervention vernacular: Clarifying meaningful differences. *NASP Communiqué, 34* (3), 1–8.

Conway, S. J., & Kovaleski, J. F. (1998). A model for statewide special education reform: Pennsylvania's Instructional Support Teams. *International Journal of Educational Reform, 7,* 345–351.

Dana, N. F., & Yendol-Silva, D. (2003). *The reflective educator's guide to classroom research: Learning to teach and teaching to learn throughpractitioner inquiry.* Thousand Oaks, CA: Corwin Press.

Deno, S. (1970). Special education as developmental capital. *Exceptional Children, 37,* 229–237.

Deno, S. (2003). Development of curriculum-based measurement. *Journal of Special Education, 37*(3), 184–192.

Deno, S., & Mirkin, P. (1977). *Data-based program modification.* Paper presented at the meeting of the Council for Exceptional Children, Reston, VA.

Denton, C. A. (Ed.). (2006). Responsiveness to intervention as an indication of learning disability [Theme issue]. *Perspectives. 32*(1).

Dole, J. (2004). The changing role of the reading specialist in school reform. *Reading Teacher, 57*(5), 462–471.

Education of All Handicapped Children Act of 1975. (1975). 20 U.S.C. 33 Section 1400 *et seq.*

Fletcher, J. M., Denton, C., & Francis, D. J. (2005). Validity of alternative approaches for the identification of learning disabilities: Operationalizing unexpected underachievement. *Journal of Learning Disabilities, 38,* 545–552.

Fletcher, J. M., Lyon, G. R., Fuchs, L. S., & Barnes, M. A. (2007). *Learning disabilities: From identification to intervention.* New York: Guilford Press.

Flugum, K. R., & Reshly, D. J. (1994). Prereferral interventions: Quality indices and outcomes. *Journal of School Psychology, 32*(1), 1–14.

Florida Department of Education (2004a). *Improving student learning through classroom action research.* Tallahassee: Author.

Florida Department of Education. (2004b). Summative report of effective instructional practices project. Tallahassee: Author.

Foorman, B. R., Francis D. J., Fletcher, J. M.., Schatschneider, C., & Mehta, P. (1998). The role of instruction in learning to read: Preventing reading failure in at-risk children. *Journal of Educational Psychology, 90,* 37–55.

Fuchs, D., & Deshler, D. (2007). What we need to know about responsiveness to intervention (and shouldn't be afraid to ask). *Learning Disabilities Research & Practice. 22,* 129-136.

Fuchs, D., & Fuchs, L. S., (1994). Inclusive schools movement and the radicalization of special education reform. *Exceptional Children, 60,* 294–300.

Fuchs, D., & Fuchs, L. S. (2005). Introduction to Response to Intervention: A blueprint for practitioners, policymakers, and parents. *Teaching Exceptional Children, 38* (1), 57–61.

Fuchs, D., & Fuchs, L. S. (2006a). Introduction to Response to Intervention: What, why, and how is it valid? *Reading Research Quarterly, 41*(1), 93-98.

Fuchs, D., & Fuchs, L. S. (2006b). Responsiveness-to-Intervention: A blueprint for practitioners, policymakers, and parents. *Teaching Exceptional Children, 38*(1), 93–98.

Fuchs, D., Mock, D., Morgan, P. L., & Young, C. L. (2002). Responsiveness to intervention: Definitions, evidence, and implications for the learning disabilities construct. *Learning Disabilities Research & Practice, 18,* 157–171.

Fuchs, L. S. (2003). Assessing intervention responsiveness: Conceptual and technical issues. *Learning Disabilities Research and Practice, 18*(3), 172–186.

Fuchs, L. S., Fuchs, D., Hamlett, C. L., Hope, S. K., Hollenbeck, K. N., Capizzi, A., et al. (2006). Extending responsiveness-intervention to math problem-solving at third grade. *Teaching Exceptional Children, 38*(4), 59–63.

Fuchs, L.S., Fuchs, D., Hamlett, C.L., Walz, L., & Germann, G. (1993). Formative evaluation of academic progress: How much growth can we expect? *School Psychology Review, 22,* 27–48.

Fullan, M. (2005, December). *Tri level reform.* Paper presented at meeting of the National Staff Development Council, Vancouver, BC.

Gersten, R., & Dimino, J. A. (2006). RtI (Response to intervention): Rethinking special education for students with reading difficulties (yet again). *Reading Research Quarterly, 41*(1), 99–108.

Glanz, J. (2003). *Action research: An educational leader's guide to school improvement.* Norwood, MA: Christopher-Gordon.

Good, R. H., & Kaminski, R. A. (Eds.). (2002). *Dynamic indicators of basic early literacy skills* (5th ed.). Eugene, OR: Institute for the Development of Educational Achievement.

Gresham, F. (1989). Assessment of treatment integrity in school consultation and prereferral intervention. *School Psychology Review, 18*(1), 37–50.

Gresham, F., MacMillan, D. L., Beebe-Frankenberger, M. E., & Bocian, K. M. (2000). Treatment integrity in learning disabilities intervention research: Do we really know how treatments are implemented? *Learning Disabilities Research and Practice, 15*(4), 198–205.

Grimes, J., & Kurns, S. (2003, December). *An intervention-based system for addressing NCLB and IDEA expectations: A multiple tired model to ensure every child learns.* Paper presented at the National Research Center on Learning Disabilities Responsiveness-to-Intervention Symposium, Kansas City, MO.

Guskey, T. (2000). *Evaluating professional development.* Thousand Oaks, CA: Corwin Press.

Guskey, T. R., & Sparks, D. (1996). Exploring the relationship between staff development and improvements in student learning. *Journal of Staff Development*, 17(4), 2–6.

Hallahan, D. P., Keller, C. E., McKinney, J. D., Lloyd, J. W., & Bryan, T. (1988). Examining the research base of regular education initiative: Efficacy studies and the adaptive learning environments model. *Journal of Learning Disabilities, 21,* 29–35, 55.

Harp, B. (2000). *The handbook of literacy assessment and evaluation.* Norwood, MA: Christopher-Gordon.

Henson, K. T. (1996). Teachers as researchers. In J Sikula, et al. (Eds.). *Handbook of research on teacher education* (2nd ed., pp. 53–64). New York: Simon & Schuster Macmillan.

Hirsh, S. (2004). Putting comprehensive staff development on target. *Journal of Staff Development*, 25(1), 12–15.

Hubbard, R. S., & Power, B. M. (1993). *The art of classroom inquiry: A handbook for teacher-researchers.* Portsmouth, NH: Heinemann.

Hubbard, R. S., & Power, B. M. (1999). *Living the questions: A guide for teacher-researchers.* Portland, ME: Stenhouse.

Idol, L., Paolucci-Whitcomb, P., & Nevin, A. (1986). *Collaborative consultation.* Rockville, MD: Aspen.

Ikeda, M. J., & Gustafson, J. J. (2002). *Heartland AEA 11's problem-solving process: Impact on issues related to special education.* (Research Rep. No. 2002-01). Johnson, Iowa: Heartland Area Education Agency.

Individuals With Disabilities Education Act of 1997. (1997). 20 U.S.C. 33 Section 1400 *et seq.*

Individuals With Disabilities Education Act of 2004. (2004). 20 U.S.C. 33 Section 1400 *et seq.* Retrieved August 30, 2007, from www.ed.gov/policy/apeced/guid/idea2004.html

International Reading Association. (2006). *New roles in response to intervention: Creating success for schools and children.* Newark, DE: Author.

Jankowski, E. A. (2003, Fall). Heartland Area Education Agency's problem-solving model: An outcomes-driven special education paradigm. *Rural Special Education Quarterly.* Retrieved July 25, 2007, from www.findarticles.com/p/articles

Jimerson, S. R., Burns, M. K., & VanDerHeyden, A. (Eds.) (2007). *Handbook of response to intervention: The science and practice of assessment and intervention.* New York: Springer.

Kavale, K. A., & Forness, S. R. (2000). History, rhetoric, and reality. *Remedial and Special Education, 21,* 279–297.

Kelly, M., & Rawlinson, D. (2003). *Action Research.* Tallahassee: Florida Department of Education.

Killion, J. (2005). *Assessing impact: Evaluating staff development.* Oxford, OH: National Staff Development Council.

Lau, M., Sieler, R., Muyskens, P., Canter, A., VanKeuren, T., & Marston, D. (2006). Perspectives on the use of the problem-solving model from the viewpoint of school psychologist, administrator, and teacher. *Psychology in the Schools, 43*(1), 117–127.

Lenz, B. K., & Deshler, D. D. (2004). *Teaching content to all: Evidence-based inclusive practices in middle and secondary schools.* Boston: Allyn & Bacon.

Little, M. (2001). Classroom action research improving student outcomes. *Florida Educational Leadership, 2*(1), Sept., 41–44.

Little, M. (2003). Professional development to improve student learning: A systems approach. In E. M. Guyton & J. Dangle (Eds.) *Teacher education yearbook XII: Research linking teacher preparation and student performance* (pp. 57–82). Dubuque, IA: Kendall/Hunt.

Little, M. (2004). Professional development to improve student learning: A systems approach. In E. M. Guyton & J. Dangle (Eds.) *Teacher Education Yearbook XII: Research Linking Teacher Preparation and Student Performance* (pp. 57–82). Dubuque, IA: Kendall/Hunt.

Little, M., & Houston, D. (2003). Research into practice through professional development. *Remedial & Special Education, 24*(2), 75–88.

Marston, D., Muyskens, P., Lau, M., & Canter, A. (2003). Problem-solving model for decision making with high-incidence disabilities: The Minneapolis experience. *Learning Disabilities Research & Practice, 18,* 187–200.

McLeskey , J., & Skiba, R. (1990). Reform and special education: A mainstream perspective. *Journal of Special Education, 24,* 319–326.

McMaster, K. L., Fuchs, D., Fuchs, L. S., & Compton, D. L. (2003, December). *Responding to non-responders: An experimental field test of identification and intervention methods.* Paper presented at the National Research Center on Learning Disabilities Responsiveness-to-Intervention Symposium, Kansas City, MO.

National Association of School Psychologists. (2006). *Problem solving and RtI: New roles for school psychologists*. Retrieved August 30, 2007 from www.nasponline.org

National Association of State Directors of Special Education. (2005). *Response to intervention: Policy considerations and implementation*. Reston, VA: Author.

National Council of Teachers of Mathematics. (2003). *Principles and standards for school mathematics*. Reston, VA: Author.

National Institute for Literacy (2007). *Response to intervention: Policy considerations and implementation*. Retrieved August 30, 2007, from www.nifl.gov/partnershipforreading/publications.html

National Research Center on Learning Disabilities (2006). Core concepts of RtI. Retrieved July 25, 2007, from www.nrcld.org.

National Staff Development Council (2000). *Standards for professional development*. Oxford, OH: Author.

No Child Left Behind Act (2002). Public Law 107-220. 107th Congress. Full text: http://www.ed.gov/legislation/ESEA02/.

Pascopella, A. (2003). The next challenge. *District Administrator, 39*(6), 24–29.

President's Commission in Excellence in Special Education (2002). *A new era: Revitalizing special education for children and their families*. Retrieved July 27, 2007, from www.ed.gov/inits/commissionboards/index.html.

Reschly, D. J., & Graham, F. M. (2006, April). *Implementation fidelity of SLD identification procedures*. Presentation at the National SEA Conference on SLD Determination: Integrating RTI within the SLD Determination Process, Kansas City, MO. Retrieved July 12, 2007, from www.nrcld.org/sea/presentations_worksheets/fidelity/Reschly.pdf&

Reschly, D. J., & Hosp, J. L. (2004). State SLD identification policies and practices. *Learning Disabilities Quarterly, 27*(4), 197-213.

Robertson, C. & Salter, W. (1995a). *The Phonological Awareness Kit: Primary*. East Moline, IL: LinguiSystems.

Robertson, C. & Salter, W. (1995b). *The Phonological Awareness Profile*. East Moline, IL: LinguiSystems.

Sagor, R. (2005). *How to conduct collaborative action research*. Alexandria, VA: Association for Supervision and Curriculum Development.

Salvia, J., & Ysseldyke, J. (1998). *Assessment*. Boston: Houghton Mifflin.

Schmuck, R. A. (1997). *Practical action research for change*. Arlington Heights: IL: IRI SkyLight.

Shapiro, E.S. (1996). *Academic skills problems: Direct assessment and interventions*. New York: Guilford Press.

Stiggins, R. J. (1997). *Student-involved classroom assessments*. Columbus, OH: Merrill Prentice Hall.

Tilly, D. (2003). *Results of a 3-tiered model implementation: The Heartland Early Literacy Project*. Paper presented at the National Research Center on Learning Disabilities "Responsiveness to Intervention" Symposium, Kansas City, MO. Retrieved July 13, 2007, from www.nrcld.org/symposium2003/tilly/tilly8.html.

Torgesen, J. (2003). O*perationalizing the response to intervention model to identify children with learning disabilities*. Paper presented at the National Research Center on Learning Disabilities "Responsiveness to Intervention" Symposium, Kansas City, MO. Retrieved July 13, 2007, from www.nrcld.org/symposium2003/tilly/tilly8.html.

U. S. Department of Education Office of Special Education and Rehabilitative Services. (2006). *A new era: Revitalizing special education for children and their families.* Washington, D.C: Author. Retrieved August 7, 2007, from http://www.ed.gov/inits/commissionsboards/whspecialeducation/

Vaughn, S. (2003, December). *How many tiers are needed for response to intervention to achieve acceptable prevention outcomes.* Paper presented at the National Research Center on Learning Disabilities "Responsiveness to Intervention" Symposium, Kansas City, MO. Retrieved July 13, 2007, from www.nrcld.org/symposium2003/tilly/tilly8.html.

Vellutino, F. R., Scanlon, D., Small, S., & Fanuele, D. (2006). Response to intervention as a vehicle for distinguishing between children with and without reading disabilities: Evidence for the role of kindergarten and first-grade interventions. *Journal of Learning Disabilities, 39,* 157–169.

Villa, R. A., & Thousand, J. (1996). Teacher and administrator perceptions of heterogeneous education. *Exceptional Children, 63,* 29–46.

Wagner, R. K., Torgesen, J. K., Rashotte, C. A., Hecht, S. A., Barker, T. A., Burgess, S., et al. (1997). Changing causal relations between phonological processing abilities and work-level reading as children develop from beginning to fluent readers: A five-year longitudinal study. *Development Psychology, 33,* 468–479.

Wiggins, G. (1998). *Educative assessment: Designing assessments to inform and improve student performance.* San Francisco: Jossey-Bass Inc.

Wright, J. (2007). RTI Team Teacher Referral Form (Exhibit 3B). *RTI toolkit: A practical guide for schools.* Port Chester, NY: National Professional Resources.

Index

McMaster, K. L., 27
Minneapolis Public Schools, 27
Mirkin, P., 9, 15, 27
Mock, D., 1
Morgan, P. L., 1
Moultrie, R., 9
multi-disciplinary teams. *See* collaboration
Muyskens, P., 27, 32

N

National Association of State Directors of Special Education, 10
National Center on Progress Monitoring, 42
National Council of Teachers of Mathematics (NCTM), 51–52, 55
National Institute for Literacy, 42
National Research Center on Learning Disabilities, 42
National Staff Development Council (NSDC), 20
Nevin, A., 19
No Child Left Behind (NCLB), 7–8, 15, 41
norm-referenced tests, 53

O

observations, 52, 97–99
Office of Special Education Programs (OSEP), 48

P

Paolucci-Whitcomb, P., 19
Pascopella, A., 7
permanent product assessment, 53
portfolios, 55
Power, B. M., 20, 54
prereferral team, 61
President's Commission on Excellence in Special Education, 9
problem identification, 34–40, 59, 69–70, 80, 87–88, 90–91, 105
        probes for, 36–39
problem statement, 39, 70
professional development, 2, 9, 20, 22–23, 29–30, 45, 60–61
progress monitoring. *See* assessment
Pysh, M. V., 9

R

reflective practice, 17
reform, 18
Regular Education Initiative (REI), 8
Reschly, D. J., 9, 42

Research Institute on Progress Monitoring, 42
research question, 43–45, 70
robust indicators, 42–43
rubrics, 55

S

Sagor, R., 34, 51, 53, 61
Salvia, J., 53
Scanlon, D., 27
Schmuck, R. A., 20
screening, universal, 6
Shores, C., 28
Sieler, R., 32
Small, S., 27
special education
        discrepancy model, 8
        eligibility, 1–2, 8, 11, 13–14, 18, 25
        history, 8–9
        identification, 6, 8
        misdiagnosis, 6
        referrals (placement), 9, 27, 59
        service delivery models of, 8
standard protocol model, 27–28
Stein, 15
student learning. *See* assessments, progress monitoring
student work, 54–55
student
        achievement, 1–2, 47
        characteristics of, 40
        demographics of, 11
        with disabilities (SWD), 7
        goals for, 2, 39, 41, 45–46, 57, 60
        instructional needs of, 5
        rights, 8
support, 46, 48

T

teams, 26, 28–31, 76, 78
tests, 53
Thousand, J., 9
Tilly, D., 27
triangulation, 51

U

U. S. Department of Education, 47
universal instruction, 12–13
University of Kansas, 48

V

Vanderbilt University, 48
VanKeuren, T., 32